How to Be a
Property Goddess

Smita Talati

HELP YOURSELF

First published in Great Britain in 2004

British Library Cataloguing in Publication Data
A record for this book is available from the British Library

ISBN 0 340 86227 0

Typeset in ACaslonRegular by Avon DataSet Ltd,
Bidford-on-Avon, Warwickshire

Printed and bound in Great Britain by
Bookmarque Ltd, Croydon, Surrey

The paper and board used in this paperback are natural recyclable products
made from wood grown in sustainable forests. The manufacturing processes
conform to the environmental regulations of the country of origin.

Hodder & Stoughton
A Division of Hodder Headline Ltd
338 Euston Road
London NW1 3BH
www.madaboutbooks.com

Acknowledgements

Many people have helped make this book what it is. My thanks to Patrick Knowles for the fantastic covers, Sarah Dennis for her hard work in the publicity department, and Suzanne Kennedy, her predecessor, for gaining such fantastic coverage for Financial Goddess. My gratitude also to my superb agent Andrew Lownie for his hard work and loyalty.

To my father with love and gratitude.

Contents

1

Welcome to the Generation of the Property Goddesses

As the promotional face of Virgin Cola and cosmetics in the 1990s, Debbie Flett, a glamorous blonde from south London, was often mistaken for *Baywatch* babe Pamela Anderson. But behind the sweet model's smile lies a smart young businesswoman whose combination of guts, instinct and financial acumen have made her a property millionairess at the age of just thirty.

Debbie bought her first property – a two-bedroom starter house in Kingston, Surrey, for £97,500 – at the tender age of eighteen. Five years later, in 1997, she fell in love with a swanky two-bedroom apartment that was being constructed on a new development along the River Thames.

But with an off-plan price tag of £205,500, the waterside property was far beyond her means, so she took a leaf out of Richard Branson's book and resorted to an extremely high-risk strategy of raising the deposit for her second home.

She scoured the market for credit cards offering zero and low-interest introductory offers, and in total, using different credit cards, she withdrew £30,000 in cash. Many other borrowers in her situation would have become seriously unstuck, and ended up paying thousands of pounds in interest as their giddy kaleidoscope of debts spiralled way out of control.

But not Debbie. By logging all her borrowings on to a spreadsheet, she ensured the balances were transferred from one card to the next as soon as the introductory offer periods expired. Shuffling myriad different payments on different days of the month on a dazzling array of credit cards to keep interest costs to a minimum was a highly stressful juggling act, and certainly not recommended as a way of raising property finance. But not only did Debbie ensure that the gamble paid off, she also accumulated enough points on her credit cards to earn herself two free return flights to Sydney!

The secret of her success

Debbie risked borrowing heavily on credit cards to purchase her second property off-plan because she believed the riverside new-build was significantly under-priced and would increase in value once the development was completed.

And her instincts proved right. A year and a half later, she sold the flat at a substantial profit, paid off all the debt on her credit cards, and was able to put down a deposit on her third home, worth £355,000, without having to borrow a penny more.

Since then, Debbie has been investing her earnings from modelling and television work into new properties and has built up an impressive property empire. At the time of writing, she owned three luxurious apartments in west London worth more than a million pounds in total, and had plans to add three more homes to her portfolio in the coming year.

The chicks and mortar revolution

Debbie's story is impressive but not unusual, as more women than ever before are joining, and profiting from, the property market. Thirty years ago, the typical British homebuyer was a couple, and banks would take only one income into account when advancing a mortgage. Today, female first-time buyers outnumber male first-time buyers by almost two to one, and single women have become the fastest-growing group of homeowners in the UK.

The latest government statistics reveal that one in seven homebuyers in Britain are now single women, and they account for 20 per cent of all new mortgage lending. In fashionable metropolitan cities, the figures are even higher. In London, women purchase a quarter of all homes on the market, and estate agents report that they are receiving a growing number of enquiries from affluent career women looking to spend a million pounds or more on their dream home.

In the USA, the story is the same. The National Association of Realtors reports that in 2001 single women accounted for 15 per cent of all home purchases, while single men accounted for just 7 per cent of purchases. And one-tenth of all buyers of second homes in the USA are single women.

So welcome to the generation of the property goddesses – women today have become an influential force in the property market. Property developers are responding to the trend by designing more female-friendly flats and apartments, and women are likely to be key players in the housing market of the future.

Smart women buy rather than rent

The growth of the female homebuyer is partly a casualty of the high divorce rate – about half of the 90,000 women buyers in the UK each year are recently separated or bereaved – but, more largely, it is a reflection of social and economic change.

For the first time ever in Britain, there are more women than men training to become accountants and lawyers, and the number of women entering higher education now exceeds the number of men by a considerable margin. Women graduates are rising up the career ladder younger and faster than ever before. They are breaking through the proverbial 'glass ceiling' and reaching the highest echelons of success in banking, commerce, new technology, film, music and the media.

And much of this new female wealth is being directed into the property market, as women aspire to the security and investment of home ownership. Young men might be happy to continue renting shared bachelor flats well into their thirties and forties, but with the average British home doubling in value every seven years, smart women know that they are far better off buying. So, as soon as they settle into their first well-paid job, they start saving up for a deposit, phoning estate agents, and looking for their first home.

The women homebuyers

According to Bradford & Bingley's *Home Report*, the three things women look for when buying property are: security, proximity to transport, and tasteful décor.

Female buyers take a keen interest in the financial and budgeting process of buying a home, and once they find a property that meets their requirements, they tend to proceed swiftly and efficiently with the purchase. On the other hand, estate agents report that male buyers tend to be more ambiguous about what they are looking for, have to be dragged along to viewings, and prove less flexible when it comes to negotiating the deal!

The deluge of property makeover programmes in recent years has whetted the nation's appetite for snapping up a wreck and transforming it into a sumptuous home. But even in the traditionally male-dominated industry of property development, findings show that women who buy a property 'in need of modernisation' are more likely to see the project through than male buyers.

Ian Dickson, of Winkworth's estate agents in Shepherd's Bush, west London, says: 'We see a lot of male buyers selecting properties with potential for improvement, but very often when we go to revalue the properties two years later, we find that none of the work has actually been carried out. However, women are much more organised and realistic about what they are hoping to achieve.'

Even if they don't buy a renovation property, today's canny female homeowners are keen to add value to their properties. Forget the tired image of the high-maintenance girl-about-town frittering away all her spare cash on coats, shoes and matching handbags. Come the weekend, today's smart career woman would much rather be shopping at Homebase or Do It All than Zara or TopShop! A recent survey by the Alliance

& Leicester revealed that women in their thirties have become Britain's most avid DIY enthusiasts, spending more money on home improvements each year than men of all ages.

Property and the Victorian woman

However, the doors to the property-owning club have not always been open to females. Back in early nineteenth-century England, the law regarded women as too emotional, irresponsible and incompetent to manage real estate, so married women were not legally entitled to own homes or personal wealth, and were forced to relinquish any assets they had inherited to their husbands. Their estates became absorbed into the marriage, and they had no rights to file for divorce.

Marriage and property are recurring themes in the great Victorian novels, which were written at a time when women's property rights were being hotly debated and challenged in society. Caroline Norton, a popular poet, novelist and beautiful socialite, proved to be an important catalyst for reform.

In 1836, Caroline attempted to separate from her husband on the grounds of cruelty, but her claim was rejected by the courts. Severed of financial support, and denied access to her home and her children, she began writing to support herself. In 1855, she published her most important pamphlet, *A letter to the Queen on Lord Cranworth's Marriage and Divorce Bill*.

It proved influential, and two years later a new Act was established, granting property rights to wives separated from their husbands. However, the financial status of married women did not improve significantly until 1882, when a second Married Women's Property Act, mandating that married women could keep all personal and real property they acquired before and during marriage, came into force.

Buying your first home today

Every woman today aspires to owning a home that is secure, comfortable and beautiful, whether she buys alone, or with a husband, partner, sibling or friend. Not every woman has the nerve or the desire to become a high-gambling property investor like Debbie, but provided you buy a decent property in a good location and maintain it well, a home should prove to be one of the best investments you make in your lifetime.

But while more women are joining the property market for the first time than ever before, there is no doubt that buying a first home today is a veritable financial challenge. Stratospheric price rises in recent years mean that a vast number of young professionals across the UK have become priced out of the property market. The problem is particularly acute in London where, by January 2004, the price of the average first home had leapt to £160,000, and the number of first-time buyers plummeted to an all-time low.

However, the good news is that first-time buyers are crucial to the lifeblood of the property market, and mortgage lenders, property developers and local authorities are responding to the crisis by making a gamut of innovative mortgage products and affordable homes available to cash-strapped young buyers. In Chapter 2, we will explore how to take advantage of shared-ownership schemes, buy property with friends or siblings, find innovative mortgage products, and even receive cashbacks from property developers to buy a brand-new home, to help you turn the dream of home ownership into reality.

Buying and selling is stressful

But there are many other factors and variables other than price that today conspire to make buying and selling property and moving home an often difficult and stressful experience.

First, there is a severe shortage of all types of desirable housing in Britain across all prices brackets, so whether you are looking for your first one-bedroom flat in Manchester or a million-pound detached family house in Surrey, finding that dream property is likely to be a competitive business, one that will require full commitment on your part.

Second, the current system of purchasing a home in England and Wales is highly cumbersome and inefficient. Buyers cannot be sure if the property they are about to purchase has a good title, is structurally secure, or is standing next door to a future petrol station, until they have carried out and paid for the necessary searches and surveys – and most buyers, quite understandably, do not want to do this until *after* their offer on the property has been accepted.

The average property transaction takes thirteen weeks to reach completion, and each year a third of all property sales collapse halfway through the process, causing much grief to buyers and sellers who need to move home in order to get on with their lives.

Home Information Packs

The good news is that thanks to a new Housing Bill having been passed in Parliament in November 2003, this absurd housebuying system is in the process of being revolutionised.

As of January 2006, sellers will be legally obliged to provide buyers, at the viewing stage, with comprehensive 'Home Information Packs' that will contain all the vital information about a property that they need to know. This will include: title deeds, local authority searches, building regulations' consents, warranties and guarantees for major works carried out, information about standard questions such as fixtures and fittings to be included in the sale, or problems with neighbours, etc. Vendors of leasehold flats will have to provide full details of the property's lease, ground rent and service charges. All sellers will also have to provide in their packs an independent 'home condition report', similar to the current homebuyer's survey.

This should help speed up the process of buying a property and reduce the number of sales that fall through, as buyers will be provided with a much fuller picture of the property they intend to buy before putting in an offer. It will also reduce the initial costs of purchasing a home for first-time buyers who have nothing to sell.

The right way to buy and sell

Until the Bill takes effect, buying a property in England and Wales will continue to be a bit like shopping in the dark, as buyers only have limited information about the property they are making an offer on. The aim of this book is to help mitigate the chances of a house sale going pear-shaped, and maximise your chances of profiting from the market, by providing straightforward advice on the right way to go about buying, selling and moving home.

The five commandments of the property goddess

Each of the following chapters will provide a step-by-step guide to buying and selling a home, becoming a property investor, and buying a property abroad. But first, there are 'five commandments' that every property goddess should familiarise herself with. Whether buying a property at home or abroad, for nesting or investing, you must:

1 Decide what you are looking for in a dream home.
2 Work out your budget and get a mortgage offer agreed in principle.
3 Ensure that you are 100 per cent ready to buy.
4 Add value to your property/properties.
5 Sell quickly and profitably.

1 Decide what you are looking for in a dream home

Poring over glossy property supplements and peering into estate agents' windows as you wander down the high street is a national pastime. But waltzing out on to the streets in search of a dream home without actually sitting down and thinking about what you want in terms of location, room proportions, storage space, light, living, cooking and entertaining space will at best be a total and utter waste of time, and at worst could result in you buying a property that is totally unsuitable for your needs. So before registering with every estate agent in sight, draw up a list of the key things you are looking for in a new home. This should include:

- where you want to live – e.g. location, location, location!
- the number of bedrooms and bathrooms you need;
- the size and layout of kitchen you require;
- whether you'd like a garden, garage, or some outdoor space;
- how much space and natural light you need in each room.

Within these categories you are likely to have numerous other preferences. For example, if you are looking for a family home, you might want a property with a south-facing garden. If you drive an expensive car, you might want off-street parking. If you are planning to rent out a second bedroom, an en-suite bathroom might come in handy.

Having drawn up an extensive wish list of your desires and requirements, split them up into three different columns:

essential criteria that you will not compromise on (e.g. quiet residential street, close to public transport); those things you might be willing to compromise on (e.g. décor, style of kitchen and bathroom); and those things that are absolutely unacceptable (e.g. basement flats, galley kitchens that do not have room for all the essential fixtures and fittings).

You are highly unlikely to find the perfect property, but drawing up checklists will help you and your estate agent clarify what you are looking for, ensure that you do not waste time viewing unsuitable properties and, equally importantly, do not allow your judgment to be swayed by clever décor, lighting and use of furniture.

2 Work out your budget and get a mortgage offer agreed in principle

Having decided what you're looking for in your dream home, your next job is to work out exactly how much you have to spend, and to get a *mortgage offer agreed in principle*. The latter point is extremely important because your third commandment is to ensure that by the time you get round to making an offer on a property, you are *100 per cent ready* to buy it, and if you're still waiting for a mortgage approval to come through two weeks after putting in your bid, you'll fall short here.

There are thousands of different mortgage products out there: fixed, discounted, capped, tracker rates for one, two, three, five, ten or even twenty-five years. But a low-rate loan that gives you the flexibility to switch to a better deal without penalty will save you literally thousands of pounds over the life of your mortgage, so it's important to choose your loan with care, and *keep it under review*.

You'll get a much better mortgage deal if you can put down a deposit of at least 5 per cent of the purchase price of your property. However, raising a sufficiently large deposit is often the biggest hurdle for the first-time buyer. If you are confident that the property you want to buy will hold its value in the short term, you might want to consider taking out a 100 per cent mortgage.

If you are buying a leasehold flat, you will have to pay ground rent and service charges, which can add a couple of thousand pounds a year to your annual bill on top of mortgage payments, so don't forget to factor these into the equation when working out your budget. You will also need to budget for buildings' and contents' insurance.

Other costs of buying

Aside from the deposit, you will also have to meet numerous other expenses associated with buying a home. The Inland Revenue levies stamp duty of between 1 per cent and 4 per cent on properties over £60,000. Until the new Home Information Packs come into force in January 2006, you will also have to pay for a structural survey and local authority searches, as well as the solicitor's fees to cover the legal costs of purchasing a home. In total, buying a £150,000 flat is likely to cost about £2,500 in stamp duty, surveys and legal fees, while buying a £500,000 house could set you back well over £16,000 in these extra costs.

The cost of trading up

And if you thought buying your first property was expensive, take a deep breath if you're looking to trade up. Hopefully, you will have built up equity in the market, so the deposit should not be a problem. But this time around, you will have to meet the costs of selling your existing home, as well as buying your next one.

In total, trading up from a £200,000 property to a £300,000 one is likely to set you back more than £13,000 in legal fees, stamp duty, estate agents' commission, surveys and searches, while trading up from a £300,000 home to a £500,000 one could end up costing you a cool £40,000!

One of the reasons there has been so much apathy from estate agents for the new Home Information Packs is that they will make selling a property even more expensive. It is estimated that the cost of putting together a Home Information Pack will be about £700. However, as most people who are selling a property will also be buying another one, they will be able to claw back this money by saving on the cost of surveys and searches on their next place, so this argument is flawed.

Save thousands of pounds when selling by being your own estate agent

By far the biggest expense involved in moving home is using an estate agent to sell your property. A typical estate agent will take commission of at least 1.5 per cent of the eventual sale price if they find a buyer for you. If you decide to market your property with more than one estate agent, the fee can be as high as 3 per cent of the sale price. So using an estate agent to sell a £200,000 property could end up costing you £6,000 in commission alone, which is why – in Chapter 3 – I encourage every property goddess to cut out the middleman and sell her home herself.

Getting the sums right when doing buy-to-let

If you are keen to follow Debbie's example and become a property investor, it is even more crucial to work out your finances carefully and build in *a contingency fund*. Far too many people have jumped on the property investment bandwagon in recent years expecting to be able to 'get rich quick' in return for doing little more than collecting the monthly rent.

This is a fallacy. In many parts of the UK, the rental market is overflowing with vacant properties, and it can be very difficult to find tenants. Even if you do manage to let your property, every investor experiences a few void periods when they don't have tenants paying them rent, but they still have to pay the mortgage and keep the property in good repair.

Make no mistake: being a property investor is expensive, time-consuming and *very hard work*. In Chapter 5 I will show you how to get started by explaining how to work out the potential *income* and *capital* yields to determine whether a property really will make a good rental investment. I will also explain how to find good tenants, keep your property in good repair, and take advantage of new tax rules that will allow buy-to-let investors to add residential property to their pension portfolios.

3 Ensure that you are 100 per cent ready to buy

Once you have drawn up a checklist of what you are looking for in a home, worked out how much you have to spend, and obtained a mortgage offer in principle, you are 100 per cent ready to purchase your first home.

If you are moving up the ladder, the biggest conundrum you will face is figuring out whether to buy or sell first. For reasons that I will explain in much more detail in Chapter 3, the property goddess *always* sells her existing home *before* buying her next one. This way, she ensures that by the time she comes round to making an offer, she is 100 per cent ready to buy her next property.

This is important, because it is a peculiar quirk of the homebuying system in England and Wales that the sale of a property is not legally binding until the buyer and seller have exchanged contracts. So, under the current system, once your offer on a property has been accepted, you need to proceed *very quickly* with the business of getting surveys and searches carried out and finalising your financial arrangements, so that you can get to the stage of exchanging contracts as soon as possible.

If during this busy time you are also trying to spruce up your home for the market, find a buyer, and get your mortgage arranged, you will certainly cause delays, and your vendor (who is probably relying on exchanging contracts with you to buy somewhere else herself) may (quite rightly) become nervous about your commitment and ability, and accept an offer from a more organised buyer. If this happens, you will lose out on your dream home and have to commence your search all over again.

As I said, each year a third of all property sales in England and Wales fail to reach the completion stage, costing buyers and sellers a total of £350 million. Witnessing a house sale fall through is one of the most stressful experiences you can go through in the property game. So if you only take one piece of advice from this book, ensure that before putting in an offer on a home, you: a) have your existing home on the market (and preferably under offer); b) have a mortgage offer agreed in principle; and c) have a solicitor and surveyor lined up, so that if your offer is accepted you really are 100 per cent ready to go ahead and buy it.

4 Add value to your property/properties

One of the joys of owning a home is that you can decorate and furnish it in the way that you please. Every woman naturally wants her home to reflect her own sense of style, but no matter how much you love your home, sooner or later the time will come when you will want to move on, and your ability to sell your home quickly and profitably (the fifth commandment of the property goddess) will depend very much on how closely your home matches the expectations of buyers.

So, your fourth commandment is to maintain your property and make improvements that will *add value* to your home once you throw open the doors to the great buying public. Of course, nobody should make major changes to their home that they really don't like or want for the sole purpose of adding value to it (unless the property in question happens to be an investment purchase, in which case your tastes are irrelevant). But nor should you become so carried away with your love of exotic Moroccan interiors, or minimalist Japanese décor, that buyers with more conservative tastes cannot imagine living in your home.

Use neutral colours, and maximise on light and space

The key to securing a quick sale is to make your home appeal to as wide a range of buyers as possible, and the best way of doing this is to select neutral colours and classic designs for walls, floors, kitchen and bathroom units, and give your home individual character and flair by making stylish use of accessories, lighting and furniture.

When it comes to major home improvements, remember that the two things every modern homeowner craves is more *space* and *light*. A recent survey found that 17 per cent of people looking to move wanted more space. So, bright loft conversions, extra bedrooms and bathrooms, and airy, open-plan living rooms will invariably add more value to a property than cosmetic improvements such as swimming pools, fitted home offices, and even new kitchen and bathroom suites.

Don't 'do-it-yourself', unless you really know how

Given the coterie of high-profile female developers gracing our television screens on an almost nightly basis, it can be very empowering to picture yourself knocking down kitchen walls, replastering ceilings, tiling bathrooms and rewiring derelict properties.

But before you start donning hard hats and boots, be honest about your knowledge and abilities. Few things make estate agents and buyers cringe more than over-zealous DIY enthusiasts whose attempts at home improvements display all the skill and polish of a non-creative would-be *Blue Peter* presenter!

If you really don't have the time, knack and desire to carry out the required work to a sufficiently high standard, then pay somebody who does. It will be less stressful (and less expensive) in the long run, and you'll derive far more pleasure from the finished product.

Get prepared: the property goddess's little black book

Of course, we're all familiar with the horror stories of rogue builders who fix doors the wrong way round, and damp-proof contractors who tell you your house is about to sink under, in order to secure some work. But for every fly-by-night clown, there is a reliable tradesman or tradeswoman out there who will do a professional job for a fair price. The problem is finding them!

So one of your most important jobs as a property goddess is to build up a little black book containing the contact numbers of your most trusted builders, architects, plumbers, electricians, window fitters and decorators. Ask friends, family, neighbours and local estate agents for recommendations. If they can't help, contact the relevant professional bodies listed in the Appendix at the back of this book.

Plan ahead and don't get ripped off

A recent survey found that tradesmen regularly overcharge women homeowners for everything from routine plumbing jobs to major building works, so before commissioning a tradesman obtain at least three different quotes, and be prepared to bargain hard. Get the project and all the costs agreed in writing, and plan ahead. Such is the demand for decent tradespeople these days that the unspoken rule of the business is: if they're available tomorrow, they're probably not that good!

5 Sell quickly and profitably

If you buy a sensible property in a good location, maintain it well and add value to it, you should have no problem fulfilling the fifth commandment of the property goddess: to sell your home *quickly* and *profitably* when you want to move.

Being able to secure a quick sale is very important, so no matter how eager you are to move, don't be tempted to put your home on the market until you have cleaned, de-cluttered and repainted the property, so it really cries out with the 'wow factor'. But you must also be fully prepared for an avalanche of buyers to start flooding through the door, criticising your beloved home and finding reasons to negotiate the price down, so don't time a house move so that it coincides with other stressful events such as your MBA exams, driving test, wedding, or the birth of a child.

Having a property sticking on the market for months on end without attracting serious offers is not only frustrating and demoralising, it also becomes increasingly more difficult to sell as the weeks tick by. Estate agents will begin to lose enthusiasm and put their energy into new instructions, and buyers will suspect that there is something wrong with your home even if there isn't.

In Chapter 3 I will show you how to prepare your property for the market, by looking at it with fresh eyes – just like you did when you first bought it – and making strategic, cost-effective changes that will entice more buyers through the door, and hopefully add hundreds or thousands of pounds to the eventual sale price.

Be your own estate agent

As I have stressed, the cheapest way of selling your home is to cut out the middleman and sell it yourself. Given the growth of property websites and the number of buyers now using the internet to find a property, it has never been easier to sell your home without an estate agent. However, it does involve time, planning and commitment.

Having obtained several free valuations from local estate agents to determine the best market price for your property, you will need to produce a brochure and/or a webpage giving all the room measurements and features of the property. You will then need to market it through the internet, classified ads and 'For Sale' boards, take calls from prospective buyers, show them around the property, and of course negotiate the deal yourself.

But despite the hard work, many vendors find that selling their home themselves not only saves them money, but is also far more enjoyable than using an estate agent. You will have lived in your home for several years and will know it better than anyone else. Selling your property yourself puts you in direct contact with buyers, and gives you far more control over the sale than relying on an estate agent.

For those who really don't have the time or inclination to do this, I will look at how to find a good estate agent in Chapter 3. And whatever option you choose, we will consider how to vet prospective buyers, so that you don't end up accepting an offer from someone who isn't 100 per cent ready to buy!

Renting

The main purpose of this book is to help you profit from property by buying, selling and investing in the market. However, while the joys and investment of homeownership are undeniable, there is no doubt that in some circumstances it is far more prudent to rent a home than buy one.

Buying and selling property is expensive, and can be stressful and time-consuming. Property is not a liquid investment that, like stocks and shares, can be sold at the drop of a hat if you need to get your hands on your capital; nor is it a consumer purchase that you can take back to the vendor and get a refund or exchange if you make a mistake. It is a long-term investment that requires serious thought and commitment.

Most students and young professionals rent flats or houses for a few years before buying their own home. Also, if you are relocating to a different part of the country or world and are unfamiliar with the local area or bureaucracy, it is sensible to rent for a few months till you find your feet. This is particularly advisable if you want to buy a property abroad, where the laws are very different to those in the UK. In Chapter 6 I provide a brief guide to buying property in the five most popular countries for British buyers of second homes: Spain, France, Italy, Portugal and the USA; and in Chapter 7 I show you how to find a good rental property in the UK and your rights and responsibilities as a tenant.

Summary

By following the five commandments, the property goddess ensures that she does not buy a property she cannot afford, and increases her chances of landing a dream home and profiting from the market. The next chapter will provide a ten-point plan to buying a home, but before reading on, ensure you hae the five commandments etched firmly in your mind each and every time you enter the property market.

1) Know exactly what you are looking for in your dream home. Think in terms of:
   a) Location: Do you want to live in the centre of the town/ city/village, or on the outskirts? Will you be disturbed by noise from traffic, aircraft, trains? How far is the nearest train station/bus stop, supermarkets, post office, doctors' surgeries? What are the crime statistics? Are there any environmental risks?

   b) Accommodation: How many bedrooms and bathrooms do you need? Do you want a garden or garage? What layout of kitchen/dining area do you want? Is there enough storage space and natural light? Will the layout and proportions of accommodation work for you?

2) Sort out your finances. Before starting to look for a property:
   a) work out how much you can afford to purchase the property and maintain it on a day-to-day basis.
   b) Find the best mortgage deal and get an offer agreed in principle.
   c) If you are selling a property, decide on the lowest offer you can accept, in order to purchase your next one.

3) Be 100% ready to buy. Before putting in an offer:
   a) Have your finances sorted.
   b) Have a solicitor/conveyancer and surveyor lined up.

4) Add value to your property. Before making any major improvements ask yourself:
   a) Will this change significantly improve my quality of life and that of future occupants, or is it just a cosmetic improvement?
   b) Does it add space and light to the property?

5) Sell quickly and profitably. Before putting your home on the market, make sure:
   a) You have thoroughly cleaned and de-cluttered to give your property the 'wow' factor.
   b) You have done your research: how does your home compare with other properties on the market in your price bracket? What will give your home the cutting edge?

2

Buying

As already mentioned in Chapter 1, the process of buying a home in England and Wales will become much quicker and cheaper once the new Home Information Packs come into force. The Office of the Deputy Prime Minister estimates that these packs, which form part of the government's new Housing Bill, will become law in January 2006. Once introduced, they will become a compulsory requirement – because if one vendor failed to produce a pack, it would cancel out the benefits to everyone else in the chain.

In this chapter I provide an easy to follow ten-point plan to finding and buying your dream home in England and Wales (Scotland operates a different scheme, as explained at the end of the chapter). When the new Home Information Packs come into force you should hopefully be able to bypass stages 7 to 9 and be in a position to exchange contracts soon after your offer on a property has been accepted.

The first-time property goddess

Hardly a day goes by when the plight of the first-time buyer does not hit the news. By March 2004, the average price paid for a first home in England and Wales was £127,000 – more than ten times the average wage of the typical first-time buyer. According to the Halifax, homes are now too expensive for first-time buyers in three-quarters of English towns and cities (not including the most expensive places such as London, Leeds and Bristol), and the average age of the first-time buyer has leapt to thirty-four.

But if you are suffering from a serious bout of property purchase envy, don't despair just yet. It *is* still possible to become a member of the property-owning club without winning the lottery or robbing the bank, by taking advantage of some of the many innovative mortgages and affordable housing options available. But before looking at these, there are a couple of things to bear in mind:

It really is now or never – buy as soon as you can afford to

It is not the purpose of this book to forecast whether prices will go up or down in the short term, or whether the property market is about to crash. But what I would say is that if you're waiting for house prices to fall far enough for you to be able to purchase your first two-bedroom flat in west London for a mere £120,000, you're likely to be in for an extremely long wait.

Property prices did fall quite significantly in several well-heeled boroughs of London during 2003 (in Kensington and Chelsea, the market fell by 16.3 per cent), but that still did not make them *cheap*. One of the underlying reasons that property has become so expensive is that due to a variety of reasons such as difficulties in obtaining planning permission and excessive red tape, there is a severe shortage of homes in Britain. The Royal Institute of Chartered Surveyors believes an extra 241,000 homes need to be built each year just to keep up with demand caused by demographic changes such as people living longer, more single-person households, and growing numbers of second-home owners. Another government report reckons that the shortage of homes has already added an average £32,000 to the price of a first-time buyer's property.

Everyone needs somewhere to live, and although new-house building is rising further up the political agenda, it will be many years before the problem is alleviated, so good advice to first-time buyers would be to forget about whether prices are going up or down in the short term and to buy as soon as you have got your finances organised and found a property you like. After all, you are joining the property market for life, not to make a quick buck overnight.

The housing market needs first-time buyers

You may not have equity in the market, but as a first-time buyer you are in an extremely powerful position compared with all the other buyers above you, due to the simple fact that you have *nothing to sell*.

Most of us need to sell our existing home to finance the purchase of our next one. But when a buyer wanting to trade up cannot sell their existing home because the person buying it from them cannot sell theirs, or their sale is being delayed, they become stuck in every homebuyer's worst nightmare – the property chain. When this happens, things grind to a halt and nobody can go anywhere.

This is where the first-time buyer comes in extremely handy. A buyer who is living in rented accommodation and is not reliant on the sale of a property to make her purchase can buy as soon as she gets her mortgage agreed and her legal work completed, and get everybody else moving again.

First-time buyers are the 'feeders' of the property market – without them, the market would simply dry up. But giddy price rises in the past few years mean that the number of first-time buyers is now at an all-time low. Traditionally, first-time buyers have accounted for about a half of all buyers with a mortgage; however, by 2003, they had declined to just 29 per cent of the market and were falling further still, and if this trend continues it could have an adverse effect on the property market in years to come.

Mortgages for first-time property goddesses

Because first-time buyers are so crucial to the lifeblood of the housing market, mortgage lenders have come up with a raft of innovative loans to enable them to get on to the property ladder.

Guarantor mortgages

If your parents are willing to guarantee that they would make the repayments on your loan should you become unable to do so, you might want to consider a 'guarantor mortgage'.

To qualify for such a loan, your parents must demonstrate that they have sufficient income to service the whole of your loan in addition to any outstanding mortgages they may have on their own property. For this reason, they tend to be most popular with the offspring of retired parents who have paid off their own mortgage and are living off large pensions and investments.

In 2003, Newcastle Building Society launched a new type of guarantor mortgage under which parents need only guarantee the shortfall between the amount the buyer can borrow on their own salary multiple, and the amount they need to buy their home. So, going on the traditional model of borrowing 3.5 times her salary, a woman earning £35,000 could only obtain a mortgage of £122,500. However, if she wanted to purchase a flat for £170,000 with a 5 per cent deposit, she would be able to borrow £161,500 if her parents 'guaranteed' to meet the shortfall of £39,000.

Get a flatmate: 'rent a room' mortgage

Many first-time buyers buy two-bedroom properties and let out the second room to a friend to help pay the mortgage. The Inland Revenue allows you to earn up to £4,250 a year tax-free from letting a room, and a handful of lenders, such as the Bradford & Bingley, will take this income into consideration when working out how much they will lend.

As an example, on a salary of £25,000 the maximum you could borrow is £87,500. However, if you could demonstrate that you could let out a spare room for at least £355 a month, the lender might be prepared to advance an extra £14,875 (3.5 × £4,250), enabling you to borrow £102,375 in total.

No deposit: 100 per cent-plus mortgages

The biggest stumbling block to obtaining a mortgage for most first-time buyers is rustling up a sufficiently large deposit. Most lenders require a cash deposit of at least 5 per cent of the purchase price to qualify for a home loan, and the best deals are often reserved for those who can stump up considerably more. So, to purchase a £150,000 flat, you would need a deposit of at least £7,500, plus an extra £1,500 for stamp duty, legal fees, surveys and searches.

However, a growing number of lenders are now offering cash-strapped first-time buyers 100 per cent mortgages. One or two, such as Northern Rock, will even lend 125 per cent of the property price, enabling buyers with no savings to borrow the cost of stamp duty and legal fees and buy furniture. But this is extremely risky, as if the value of your home falls even by 1 per cent, your mortgage will be greater than the value of your home, and you will be in negative equity.

Interest rates on 100 per cent mortgages tend to be at least 0.5 per cent higher than those on deposit mortgages, and you are unlikely to be offered more than three times your salary, whereas if you could rustle up a deposit, a more traditional lender might just be prepared to stretch to a multiple of four.

Affordable housing

If an innovative mortgage will not help you on to the property ladder, consider one of the many 'affordable home' options available.

Buy a brand-new home

Just as many motorists relish the thought of being the first person to drive a brand-new car out of the garage forecourt, many homebuyers aspire to buying a new home at least once in their lifetime.

Buying a brand-new home as a first-time buyer is a great way of joining the property market. Many large developers such as Barratt, Berkeley, Bellway and Fairview Homes will offer to pay a deposit of 5 per cent or even 10 per cent on your behalf and, as we have seen in Chapter 1, if you buy off-plan in a good location, you may well find the property has increased in value by the time the building work is completed.

But in addition to the financial sweeteners, there is a gamut of other advantages to buying a brand-new property as a first-time homeowner. First, you will be able to move in as soon as the building work has been completed, so the transaction will be totally chain-free. Second, new homes must conform to the latest strict building standards regulations, and so should not require major maintenance work for several years. Third, they are likely to have sophisticated security systems, be more energy efficient, and therefore considerably cheaper to run than older homes.

New homes often also come with off-street parking, modern kitchens fully equipped with dishwashers and cookers, built-in wardrobes, carpets and curtains. Many developers will also allow buyers to make cosmetic changes to the property, select fixtures and furnishings, and throw in other goodies such as free televisions and sound systems, which will help keep down the costs for first-time buyers.

The major downside of buying a new home is that you will almost certainly get less square footage for your money than if you buy an older home, as there is no doubt that new homes are shrinking! It is also vital to research the developer thoroughly and to ensure that the home comes with an approved warranty, or you may have difficulty in obtaining a mortgage, and have little comeback if problems emerge with the structure of the building in future years.

Buy an ex-council property

In the 1980s, Margaret Thatcher, who infamously promulgated 'there is no prouder word in the English language than the word "freeholder" ', created a whole new generation of homeowners in Britain when she gave long-term council tenants the right to buy their homes from the government at substantial discounts.

Since then, over a million council homes have been sold off and are now in private hands. Ex-council flats tend to be at least 30 per cent cheaper than similar properties in private blocks in the same area, and ground rent and service charges are much lower too.

While communal areas might be basic, council properties usually offer spacious and well-planned living accommodation, particularly when compared with many ill-planned city conversion apartments. If you have your heart set on buying a property in a pricey area such as central London, then buying an ex-council property might be a good way of doing it. Many council estates now have a high proportion of privately owned homes, creating balanced social communities.

Club together and buy with a friend

Rather than wasting three-quarters of their salary on cramped one-bedroom flats in undesirable suburbs, a growing number of young women are opting to club together with friends or siblings to buy their first home.

The advantage of buying a home with someone else is that with two or three incomes combined you will be able to afford a much nicer property than if you bought alone. Most lenders will advance each party three times their salary, so two twenty-five-year-old women earning £25,000 a year each could afford to borrow £150,000 in total, compared with just over £80,000 each if they bought alone.

However, before proceeding with such an arrangement, there are a number of things that need to be discussed and finalised in writing, or the whole arrangement could end in tears. Buy the property as 'tenants in common' and use a solicitor to draw up an agreement, which stipulates the following:

- What will happen if one party wants to move out, or dies? When buying property with another person, be it a husband, sibling or friend, you both become jointly and severally liable for the mortgage. If one party defaults on the repayments, the lender can pursue the other. If this happens, will you sell the property, or will you buy the other out?
- How long do you expect the current arrangement to last? Special mortgage deals tend to run for a fixed term. If you take out a five-year fixed rate, and one of you wants to

move out before then, you might have to pay thousands of pounds in redemption penalties.

- If each party puts down different deposits, how much equity do you each own in the property? Likewise, what is the individual value of your mortgages? How will the equity be split when you sell if the property has increased in value?
- How will you split the costs of utility bills, repairs and home improvements? If one party pays for a major home improvement, will their share of the property increase?
- Day-to-day living: determine a policy for overnight guests, entertaining friends, pets, household chores and shopping, decorating and furnishing the property.

The maximum number of parties that can be entered in an agreement legally is four. However, given the complications and variables involved, many lenders are wary of lending to three or more friends buying together.

Shared ownership: part-buy, part-rent

This is a government-run scheme that enables buyers who are unable to purchase a home on the open market to acquire a share of between 25 per cent and 75 per cent in a property owned by the housing association, with a mortgage, and pay subsidised rent on the remainder.

Several schemes are in operation across the UK. Details vary, but generally shared-ownership tenants can increase the amount of equity they own in the property in 25 per cent increments, a process known as 'staircasing', until they own the home outright. When they want to move, they can either sell the property back to the housing association if it still owns a proportion of it, or sell on the open market in the usual way, if they have bought it outright.

Properties offered for shared ownership tend to be either

small houses on new estates, ex-council properties, or homes that have fallen into disrepair and been restored by the housing association.

However, demand exceeds supply. In 2001, there were 131,000 applicants chasing just 10,000 shared-ownership homes in London, and most other areas have long waiting lists.

If you are accepted on to a shared-ownership scheme, you will be subject to a bureaucratic interview in which your ability to meet rent and mortgage repayments will be assessed. You should also be aware that not all banks and building societies are prepared to advance mortgages on shared-ownership properties.

Government initiatives for first-time buyers in London

The plight of first-time buyers is rising high up the political agenda, particularly in London and the south-east where high prices are forcing 'key workers' such as teachers, nurses and policewomen to quit their jobs in the capital to the detriment of local public services.

In April 2004, the government launched a billion-pound scheme to help key workers on to the London property ladder. Full details of how the new scheme would operate were not available at the time of writing, although it had been announced that senior teachers in the capital would be able to qualify for equity loans of up to £100,000.

The ten-point plan to buying your dream home

Having identified how you are going to join the property-owning club, you want to ensure that the buying process itself is as smooth and stress-free as possible. Whether you are buying your first or your fifth home, follow our ten-point plan to finding, financing and purchasing that dream property:

1 Get prepared

As I said in Chapter 1, by the time you come to putting in an offer on your dream home, you must be *100 per cent ready to buy it*. This means that you must have a *mortgage offer agreed in principle*, and a good *solicitor* and *surveyor* lined up. If you are an existing homeowner, you should also have your current home on the market, and preferably *under offer*.

The timescale
On average it takes *six months* to complete the full process of buying a new home, from the time you start searching for your dream property to the day you move in. But that is only if you are organised and everything else moves along according to plan.

If you find yourself stuck in a slow chain, are gazumped by another buyer, or your vendor goes cold turkey and pulls out of the sale altogether, you may have to go right back to the beginning and start looking for another property, with the whole process easily ending up taking a year. So if you need to co-ordinate a house move with the start of a new job, a marriage, or the birth of a first child, plan your strategy accordingly.

The property market calendar
When deciding on your timescale, bear in mind that the property market does tend to follow a typical calendar. The market tends to pick up each year in early March as the daffodils and cherry blossoms come out, and grind to a halt in late November once the nights start drawing in at 3.45 p.m.

Families with young children tend to want to move during July or August so they can settle into their new home before the start of the autumn school term, so if you are looking to buy or sell property in this category, you really need to get cracking in the New Year. On the other hand, carefree young couples and singles often return from their summer holidays refreshed and eager for a change, so late summer can be a good time to buy and sell flats, provided you complete the move well before Christmas, by which time the market is virtually dormant.

2 Know what you are looking for in your dream home

As I said in the last chapter, the first commandment of the property goddess is to know what she is looking for in her dream home.

Location, location, location . . .

There's a very good reason why this single word is so important when it comes to buying property, which is why we need to repeat it three times.

You can rewire an old property, install gas central heating, overhaul an ageing roof, replace rotting windows, get a new kitchen and bathroom fitted, and even install a whirlpool and sauna, but you cannot physically uproot your home and move it somewhere else. So the very first thing you need to decide is *where* you want to live. I assume that you have already decided roughly where in the UK you want to buy. So when I talk about 'location', I mean ensuring that you buy in the right part of that city, town or village.

Convenience and ambience

The two things that make a great location are: *convenience* and *ambience*. 'Convenience' means having quick and easy access to essential services such as transport links, supermarkets, pharmacies, a post office, a doctor's surgery, and social and recreational facilities. 'Ambience' means getting a feel for the local community, its heritage and amenities, and deciding whether it could ever really feel like *home*.

It is particularly important that you consider these factors objectively if you are planning to relocate to a different part of the UK (or world even). How often have you heard the sad refrain 'We really should have researched the area more' from a couple of hapless Londoners who harboured such quixotic notions of 'escaping to the country' that they bought a dilapidated old rectory with no central heating or electric wiring, half a mile down a muddy lane, and an hour's drive from the nearest post office, supermarket and village pub.

As well as the practical and social issues, there are also numerous environmental issues to be considered when assessing location.

Limit your search to two locations
If you are torn between several locations, list the pros and cons of each, together with details of the type of property you could afford there. Study the list, and narrow it down to two locations. As you begin viewing properties in each area, you will get a clearer picture of which is the right location. However, viewing properties in more than two locations will become confusing and tiring, and you'll probably end up not buying anything.

Location checklist
To find your ideal location, make a note of the following points for each area you are considering buying in.

- *Transport*: If you commute to work, time the walk or drive to the station or bus stop, plus the journey into the city, and the walk to the office door. Could you do it every day in winter? Do you have to walk through a rough estate or down a dark passageway? If you will be driving into the station, is the car park safe? How much will it cost to park there all day?

- *Social and leisure amenities*: Singles and young couples without children will be attracted to areas with trendy bars, cafés, fashion shops, restaurants, cinemas and sports centres. Families look for good schools, open parks and spaces, a doctor's surgery, supermarkets, a chemist and a post office. Check that the area offers the social and leisure amenities for your lifestyle.
- *School*s: We all know that living within the catchment area of a good state school can add many tens of thousands of pounds to the value of a family home. If you are moving to a new area because of the local schools, contact the local authority first to check that there will actually be places available for your children. Also, check when entrance exams are held and offers for places made. If you are planning to educate your children privately, deliberately look for a similar home just a few streets outside the school catchment area – the difference in house prices could help fund several years of school fees!
- *Hospital*s: Living near to a good NHS hospital will also add value to a home. Sunday newspapers regularly publish good hospital guides, and if you are expecting a baby or caring for an elderly relative, it is a good idea to consult these.
- *Traffic pollution*: Your home should be a peaceful sanctuary from the outside world. If it is located on a busy main road, behind a railway line, or directly under a noisy flight path, it will detract from the quiet enjoyment of your home. One-way streets and residential areas with traffic-calming measures will be quieter than those without. If the property is located on a main road, check if traffic passes through

early in the morning, throughout the day, or late into the night.

- *Contaminated land*: Many houses are built on land that had previously been used for industrial purposes, and may still have contamination lurking on the ground. This will seriously impact on the future value of your property, and is something you should ensure that your solicitor investigates thoroughly before buying a property.

- *Environmental hazards*: Transmitters, telecommunications base stations, radioactive substances and landfill waste are all potential environmental hazards in residential areas of Great Britain today, so check for these too.

- *Flooding*: If are buying property on the coast, near to a river, or in low-lying land, check that the area is not at risk from flooding. A few years ago, several towns and villages in the lowlands of Kent and Sussex became severely flooded, causing devastation and misery to homeowners, and costing insurance companies several millions of pounds to repair and refurnish. Many of these homes are now virtually uninsurable.

- *Future developments*: Many areas have a designated use, such as retail, commercial or conservation, which will give you an idea of future developments that may appear on the scene. For example, if you buy a property situated in a designated 'commercial' area, it is not unreasonable to believe that office blocks, factories or warehouses may sprout up in years to come. If the property is located in a 'retail' area, chances are you will see new shops springing up in years to come.

Collating the information: drive around
You can collate a great deal of factual information concerning schools, shopping facilities, hospitals, crime rates in different postcodes, etc. from websites such as

www.upmystreet.co.uk. But to get a real feel for an area, spend a few hours driving around, and chatting to estate agents, local shopkeepers and residents. And, as with viewing properties, try to visit the area at different times of day, such as when schools are closing and after dark, as well as during daylight hours, so you build up a more complete picture.

Spotting up-and-coming areas: the cappuccino factor

To spot an up-and-coming area, follow the builders! If you can see smart new flats and houses being constructed, stylish shops, restaurants and bars sprouting up everywhere, and homeowners undertaking loft conversions and giving the exterior of their properties a general makeover, it's a good sign that the area is improving. The quality of life in an area is now commonly measured by its 'cappuccino factor' rating, e.g. the number of smart coffee shops it has. So, if the tatty old electrical distributor on the high street is about to be converted into a Starbucks, it's a sure sign that the area is going places!

The accommodation

Having sorted out your location criteria, draw up a checklist of the accommodation you require. The first question estate agents ask buyers when they sign up with them are: how many bedrooms do you need?

Bedrooms

You should be able to accommodate a good-sized double bed into every main bedroom – any room too small to accommodate a double bed is a single room. Single rooms can be useful for storage, use as a study/home office, nursery, or occasional guest room, but should not be counted as full bedrooms.

If the bedrooms don't have built-in storage space, will you be able to fit a large enough stand-alone wardrobe, dressing table, full-length mirror and two bedside tables? Does the main bedroom have sufficient light? If it is located at the front of the property, are you likely to be disturbed by street noise at night?

The kitchen

Kitchens are expensive to replace and often form the heart of the home for professionals who entertain frequently, and also for families with children, so this is the second most important room in the house to consider after the number of bedrooms, closely followed by the bathroom.

Even if you're more of a 'can't cook, won't cook' girl-about-town than a domestic goddess, don't buy a property that isn't kitted out with all the basics – a sink, a draining board, space for a fridge, cooker and dishwasher, and sufficient cupboards and work surfaces – or it will be difficult to resell later.

Open-plan kitchens that can double up as entertaining areas and living spaces are very popular these days, so avoid 'galley' kitchens, which are a common feature in some conversion flats. If the property does not have a separate laundry area, check that there is space for a washing machine and tumble dryer; there's nothing more irritating than having wet washing hanging around the house, particularly if you have children.

The bathroom(s)

Bathrooms are cheaper to update than kitchens, but will greatly affect your standard of living. You should have at least one bathroom for every three people living in the property, but the more the better! Even if you prefer a quick shower to a long luxurious soak, don't buy a property if the bathroom isn't big enough to accommodate a full-length bath. Again, it will be difficult to resell. Make sure there is ample storage space for towels, toiletries and cosmetics. A heated towel rail will minimise condensation in the bathroom. Check the water pressure, and make sure the loo flushes properly. The general rule regarding plumbing is that if it works, it's probably OK. Bathrooms are 'wet' rooms, so the floor should not be carpeted.

Many old Victorian terraced houses have bathrooms built on to the back of the kitchen, which is impractical for modern living. If you are thinking of buying such a property, consult a surveyor to see if a full bathroom can be installed upstairs. It will add value to the property, even if it means losing a bedroom. A downstairs cloakroom is always a welcome feature.

Storage space
Moving to a new home gives you a great opportunity to 'de-junk' a lot of the clutter you have accumulated over the years. However, most women need more storage space than they think!

You will need somewhere to hang up your coat, umbrella and briefcase, and dump your gym kit, and space to store away holiday luggage, overnight cases, skis, walking boots and tennis rackets. You will also need a good-sized utility cupboard to store bulky household appliances like vacuum cleaners, stepladders, ironing boards, buckets and mops, spare loo rolls and light bulbs. If you have young children, you will need space to park buggies, highchairs and toys.

Gardens, patios and balconies
A property with private outdoor space – even if it is just a balcony with enough room for a small table and a couple of chairs – is a great perk. If you are not particularly green-fingered, choose a property with decking or a patio rather than a lawn, which will require a weekly trim between March and October.

If the owners have cultivated borders full of beautiful flowers, shrubs and herbs, do check if they intend to leave them there, as it is not unknown for proud horticulturalists to dig up their plants and take them with them when they move! If the property has a shed, ask if they will be leaving that behind too.

Garages and parking

Properties with private garages are rare in cities like London. And if you are lucky enough to find a property with a garage it could be worth up to £20,000 more than a similar property without one. However, if you are buying a conversion flat or terraced house in a city, it is unlikely to come with off-street parking, which is a major disadvantage. Many local authorities require residents to purchase a parking permit. In some boroughs of London, these can cost more than £100 a year, and this (together with congestion charging!) should be factored into your annual budget.

Types of property

Having drawn up a list of the accommodation you require, you should think about what type of property you would like to live in. Most first-time buyers opt for flats as they are generally cheaper and easier to maintain than houses.

Buying a flat

Unless you buy a new-style commonhold flat, the major difference between buying a flat and a house lies in the ownership of the land. When you buy a house, you usually acquire the land on which your property stands. However, when you buy a leasehold flat in England or Wales, the ground is owned by a landlord and you will purchase a lease for a set number of years, in order to live in the property. Once that lease expires, ownership of the flat reverts back to the landlord and you no longer have the right to live in the property.

LEASEHOLDS

Landlords are responsible for the maintenance of the building and cleaning and running of communal areas, for which you will have to pay ground rent and service charges. The latter usually includes a contribution towards major repairs, maintenance works and buildings insurance. It may also include heating, electricity and water supply. If you buy a leasehold flat it is very important that you pay the ground rent and service charges on time, as if you default, the landlord can take you to court and repossess the property.

SERVICE CHARGES

Before buying a leasehold flat, ask to see copies of statements for service charges over the past few years. Has there been a dramatic rise in rates? What major repairs have been carried out recently? Are other flat-owners in the block happy with the way the property is being run by the landlord or managing agent?

HOW LONG DOES A LEASE LAST?

Leases run for a set number of years, and can be for as little as 15 years, to as long as 999 years. Obviously a property with a short lease is less secure than a property with a long lease, and it can be difficult to obtain a mortgage on a flat with a lease of less than 70 years. The Commonhold and Leasehold Reform Act 2002, which is explained below, has made it much cheaper and easier for lessors to extend their lease.

COMMONHOLD

Commonhold, a new reform that was fully implemented in April 2004, is based on the condominium system in the USA, and gives flat-owners much more control over how their blocks are managed and maintained.

Under the old leasehold system, landlords (or freeholders

of the property) made all the decisions regarding maintenance and repair, and the leaseholders simply had to foot the bill. However, under the new commonhold system, all flat-owners have absolute ownership of their flats, and shared ownership of communal areas.

All newly built flats operate a commonhold system. However, if you buy or are living in an older flat, you can still obtain commonhold ownership, provided that all the flat-owners in the block agree to buy out the freeholder. Even if you are unable to convert your lease to commonhold, the new commonhold reform gives you more power to challenge service charges imposed by the landlord, and gives you the right to take over management of your building. And, as I said above, it also gives you the right to extend a long lease, provided you have owned the flat for at least two years.

CONVERSION FLATS

Large period houses that have been divided up into self-contained homes are known as 'conversion flats'. They tend to have high ceilings and can offer a wealth of period features. However, many bad conversions have odd-shaped rooms, partition walls can be thin, and disturbance from neighbours can be a problem.

MANSION FLATS

Mansion flats with grand façades are common in the West End of London and cities like Bath and Edinburgh. Such properties look imposing from the outside, but can be dark and dreary inside. While the rooms usually have high ceilings, kitchens and bathrooms are often poky. Several city mansion blocks have fallen into disrepair and are being used to house single parents and tenants claiming benefits. Well-maintained mansion blocks with thick carpets, concierge, modern lifts and gardens usually have very high service charges.

PURPOSE-BUILT FLATS

Post-war purpose-built flats may not be glamorous, but they do tend to be cheaper than mansion flats. Partition walls may be thin, and the apartments lack period features, but purpose-built flats are relatively easy to maintain, and are often a good bet for first-time buyers.

BRAND-NEW DEVELOPMENTS

As I said above, there are numerous advantages to buying a brand-new flat, but it is important to research the developer carefully. A new-build property must be covered by a recognised warranty, so if the developer goes bust before the home is completed you get your deposit back or the work is completed by another developer. The warranty should also cover any faults arising after the work has been completed, usually for ten years. You are unlikely to be offered a mortgage on a new-build property without such a warranty.

Buying a house

Houses are generally more expensive than flats, but are the most popular type of accommodation in Britain – 90 per cent of homeowners live in houses.

TERRACED HOUSES

Just over a quarter of homeowners in Britain live in terraced houses. Mid-terraced houses have at least one other house adjoining the property on both sides, and are therefore more secure than end-of-terrace houses. Victorian terraced houses, which are popular in cities, rarely have driveways, so street parking can be a problem.

SEMI-DETACHED HOUSES

Two-thirds of Britain's homeowners live in semi-detached or detached houses. Semi-detached houses offer larger accommodation than terraced houses and are popular with families. However, they are less secure than terraced houses, as they can be accessed from the side.

DETACHED HOUSES

A detached house is still the ultimate dream of many British homebuyers. When living on your own plot of land, you are unlikely to be disturbed by neighbours. However, your home will also lack the 'insulation' of adjoining party walls, and hence be susceptible to a greater loss of heat. And again, as the property can be accessed from both sides, there is an increased security risk.

How long are you planning to stay?

Buying and selling property is expensive, so when drawing up your checklists also think about how long you are likely to live in your new property. The average British homeowner moves home every seven years, though younger buyers who are changing jobs, getting married and starting families may move more often. However, if you think you are likely to need to move again within a year, you might be better off renting rather than buying.

Single buyers

Studios and one-bedroom properties offer limited accommodation, so even if you are a single woman fresh out of university with little more than a suitcase full of clothes, books, and a saucepan to your name, try to buy a property with at least two bedrooms. The second room will come in handy as a guest room or study, or can be let out to a friend if you need help in paying the mortgage.

Starting a family

Most couples need to move home when starting a family. You will want a separate bedroom/nursery for your baby with space for changing and storing nappies, clothes and baby toiletries. You will also need a spacious kitchen and storage space for buggies, toys and blankets. Avoid properties with tight doorways and bathrooms that are on different levels to the bedrooms. Flats above the ground floor are not practical for young families unless they are serviced by a spacious lift.

Growing families

If you have a growing family, you might want to buy a three- or four-bedroom house and add a loft conversion for your teenage children. This is a very popular way of adding space and value to a home, and can be a lot cheaper and less unsettling than moving.

3 Organise your finances

As I said previously, the second commandment of the property goddess is to organise her finances and get a mortgage arranged in principle.

How much can you borrow?

The first thing you need to do is to work out how much you can borrow. Traditional lenders will advance a single buyer 3.5 times her salary and a couple 2.5 times their joint income. So, if you earn £35,000, you would be able to borrow a maximum of £122,500. If you had a joint income of £80,000, you would be able to borrow £200,000.

Most lenders will also require you to put down a deposit of at least 5 per cent of the property's value. So, to buy a £150,000 flat, you would need a deposit of at least £7,500, and would have to raise a mortgage for the remaining £142,500. To do this, you would need a single income of just over £40,700, or a joint income of at least £57,000. However, as we saw earlier in the chapter, there are numerous options for first-time buyers who are struggling to purchase a property based on this model.

Doing the sums when buying your second or third home

To work out how much you can afford to spend on your second or third home, deduct the value of your mortgage from the market price of your property, calculate how much you can borrow, and add the figures up.

So, if you are selling a £250,000 property and your existing mortgage is £100,000, you have £150,000 equity to put down on your next home. On a single salary of £35,000, you could borrow £122,500, and therefore view properties in the price bracket of £280,000–£300,000, with the aim of making an offer somewhere in the region of £250,000–£270,000.

If you are buying your next home with a partner, and you both have property to sell, it might be easier to sell one property first, then both move into the other. This will put you in a much stronger position to make an offer on your next home, as you will only be relying on the sale of one property to make your next purchase.

Finding the best mortgage

Finding the best mortgage from the bewildering array of products on the market can be a confusing business. Most buyers these days opt for capital repayment mortgages. This means that you pay off capital and interest each month, and will own the property outright when you reach the end of the mortgage term. When you take out a mortgage, you borrow money at a certain rate of interest. This rate could be 'fixed' for one, two, five, ten or even twenty-five years, or you could opt for a discounted rate, or a mortgage that tracks the Bank of England's base rate.

Fixed rates

Many first-time buyers opt for a low fixed-rate mortgage for the first two or three years, to help budget the cost of running a home. Fixed-rate mortgages offer security when interest rates are rising, as your monthly mortgage payments will remain the same until the fixed-rate period comes to an end.

However, if you do opt for a fixed-rate mortgage, ensure that you will not be locked into paying the lender's standard variable rate when the fixed-rate term comes to an end. Many lenders offer tempting rates as low as 1.99 per cent for one or two years, but then lock borrowers into their variable rate for the next five years. If during this lock-in period you move to another lender – or, in some cases, even move home – you will have to pay a 'redemption penalty' that is often the equivalent of three months' interest.

Discounted rates

If you believe interest rates are likely to fall over the coming months, you may wish to take advantage of a 'discounted'-rate mortgage. Discounted-rate mortgages can be as much as 2 per cent below the lender's standard variable rate, but unlike fixed-rate mortgages they will move up or down if interest rates change. Again, if you take advantage of a discounted rate, check that you will not be locked into paying the variable rate when the discounted rate comes to an end, and that there are no redemption penalties.

Tracker mortgages

As the name implies, tracker mortgages 'track' interest rate movements, so when the Bank of England lowers the rate, the mortgage rate you pay also falls, and when the Bank of England puts rates up, the rate you pay increases as well. There are hundreds of tracker mortgages on the market, and rates can be several percentage points below or above the Bank of England base rate.

Flexible mortgages

Flexible mortgages were first introduced in the late 1990s, and they allow homeowners to pay off large chunks of their mortgage early, and save themselves thousands of pounds in interest, or take 'repayment holidays'.

Several lenders now also offer all-in-one current account mortgages, which as the name implies combine your mortgage debt with your current account and savings. The advantage of having such an account is that if you deposit a large amount of savings into your current account from month to month, your overall mortgage debt will be reduced, so you pay less interest. The danger is that instead of reducing your mortgage systematically month by month, you might be tempted to spend all your income as it comes in, and still owe hundreds of thousands of pounds on your home in fifteen or twenty years' time.

Self-certification mortgages

A growing number of women these days are self-employed. In the past, lenders would require self-employed buyers to produce three years' worth of accounts and base their lending multiple on their net earnings. So if your business had a turnover of £40,000, but your net profit after business expenses was only £25,000, you would only be able to borrow £87,500. With a self-certification mortgage, a lender will allow you to state your own income without the need to produce accounts. But remember, it is illegal to state a false income on a mortgage application form, and if you deliberately inflate your income in order to obtain a large mortgage, you could be prosecuted.

The other costs in buying a home

Aside from the deposit, you will also need several thousand pounds to meet the other costs of buying a home.

Stamp duty

The government levies stamp duty of:

- 1 per cent on all property purchases from £60,000 to £249,999;
- 3 per cent on purchases over £250,000 to £499,999;
- 4 per cent on purchases above £500,000.

Legal fees

You will need to employ a solicitor to undertake all the legal work required to transfer ownership of the property from the vendor to yourself, and you should ask him to quote a flat fee for the job. Fees tend to start at around £350 plus VAT. A large number of specialist conveyancing firms have sprung up over the past few years. These firms deal purely with property transactions and can often be cheaper and more efficient than traditional solicitors, though less personal.

Surveys

There are two types of surveys: a homebuyer's survey which will cost around £400, and a more detailed structural survey which can cost more than £500. In addition to the survey, your mortgage lender might also ask you to pay for a valuation that will cost around £250.

Local authority searches

As I explained in my location checklist, it is very important to make environmental checks on the area in which you are buying and to scrutinise local planning applications to ensure that your local authority is not planning to erect a petrol station or motorway right behind your new home. To do this, your solicitor or conveyancer will need to conduct a local authority search, which will cost about £150.

Land Registry

The Land Registry is the official register of land ownership. Owners of all registered properties in the UK will have a Land Certificate or title deed detailing the size and location of the property, the details of the owner, and also any charges against the property such as a mortgage. When you buy a property, your solicitor will have to re-register it in your name, and this can cost anything from £100 to £300 depending on the value of the property.

Buildings and contents insurance

All lenders will require you to have buildings insurance in place before advancing you a mortgage. This insurance will protect you in the case of fire, floods, storms or subsidence, and should cover the structure of the property and all permanent fixtures such as baths, kitchen units, walls, fences and patios.

In addition to buildings insurance, you should also buy contents insurance to protect your possessions. Many insurers sell buildings and contents insurance as a package, and it makes sense to buy them together so that if disaster does strike, you will only have to deal with one insurer. Shop around for the best-value insurance policies on the internet, and review your policy each year.

4 Go property shopping

Having decided what you are looking for in a dream home in terms or location and accommodation, and organised your finances, you are ready to start property shopping.

The internet

As with many things these days, the internet is a very useful starting point for buying a property. Browsing through several websites will give you a good idea of what is available within your price range and allow you to compare properties in different locations, all from the comfort of your armchair.

Many websites allow you to take 'virtual tours' of the properties on sale. However, not all the information shown on websites is up to date, so you should use the internet as a starting point, rather than a substitute, for making personal contact with estate agents.

Estate agents

When introducing yourself to an estate agent, dress smartly so that you look like a buyer with money to spend. Take a copy of your mortgage offer with you, and inform the agent of your essential criteria regarding location and accommodation. This indicates that you are a serious buyer rather than a casual window shopper, and will place you at the top of the agent's list of buyers to call when they take on a hot new property. If things are a bit slow and you are not receiving regular calls from agents, put in quick, friendly calls to them yourself to get an update on what they have on their books, and to remind them that you are still looking.

Private adverts

You should also keep an eye out in local papers and property magazines for private sales. Vendors who sell their property privately save themselves several thousands of pounds in estate agents' commission and may well be prepared to pass on some of these savings to you by accepting a lower offer. The downside to buying directly from the vendor is that you yourself will have to do all the negotiations directly with them.

Direct mailing

If you are keen to buy a property in one or two particular streets in an area, consider creating some direct-mail postcards with your name and contact details, and dropping them into the owners' letterboxes. Selling a home is time-consuming, expensive and stressful, and if a vendor knows that there is a serious buyer waiting in the wings, it will save them the hassle of marketing the property, and they may well be in touch.

5 Conduct viewings

Having identified a handful of properties that fulfil your requirements, you will need to set up some viewings. If you are viewing properties in two locations initially, group them together so that you are not rushing backwards and forwards. Don't try to cram in more than four viewings in a morning, afternoon or evening, or your memory of each one will start to blur. Two heads are always better than one, so if you are buying alone, take an experienced friend or relative along with you. You should also arm yourself with:

- the full addresses of the properties you are viewing, and names of the owners, and the phone number of the estate agent if you are viewing through one;
- a local street map;
- change for parking meters;
- particulars of the properties;
- a notebook and pen;
- a mobile phone;
- your accommodation and location checklists.

First viewings

The aim of the first viewing is to evaluate if the property appeals to you; if the location is right; and if the property offers the right accommodation for your needs. First viewings should always be conducted during daylight hours.

Take a good look at the street you may soon be living in. Is it clean and well lit? Are the other properties in the street owner-occupied or let to tenants? Are they well-maintained? Is there a local neighbourhood watch?

Exterior of the property

Scrutinise the exterior of the property from the opposite side of the street, and then examine it close up. Are there any loose tiles on the roof? Are the windows double-glazed and fitted with security locks? Are they in keeping with the period style of the property? Can you see cracks in the brickwork? Are the drainpipes in good order? Does the front door have a doorbell and letterbox?

The inside

Estate agents are trained to give viewers a running commentary of the property as they show buyers around to arouse interest and detract attention from obvious and not-so-obvious flaws. It is also very easy to be seduced by the clever use of lighting and furniture. This is why it is so important to have all the requirements you noted in your accommodation checklist ingrained firmly in your mind. Look beyond the clutter and décor. You are assessing the property itself, not its contents.

After the viewing

Be sure to note down all your thoughts on the property before moving on to the next viewing. Give the estate agent some feedback as this will give them a better idea of what you are looking for.

The second viewing

If a property appeals to you and meets at least three-quarters of your main criteria, set up a second viewing. The purpose of a second viewing is to confirm your initial impressions and examine the property in closer detail and with a more critical eye.

You will want to check that the property really does meet all your accommodation requirements; to assess how much work will have to be carried out in terms of repairs and redecoration to make it your own; and whether all your furniture will fit. You will also want to decide how much you are prepared to offer the vendor.

Read the particulars of the property again and look at the notes you made after the first viewing. Then draw up a list of all the things you want to check again, or ask the owner or estate agent about the property. Try to organise the second viewing at a different time of the day to the first viewing.

6 Put in an offer

Once you have found a property you would like to buy, you need to put in an offer. If the property is being marketed through an estate agent, put the offer to them. If the vendor is selling the property privately, make your offer to them either face to face, over the phone, or by e-mail.

How much should you offer?

If the property you want to buy requires major repairs such as a new roof, new windows, new kitchen or bathroom, obtain an estimate of how much it will cost to carry out such work and deduct this from the asking price. Remember that you can always increase your offer, so start low. As a general rule, offer 10–15 per cent below the asking price in the first instance.

What happens after you put in your offer?

The estate agent will put your offer to the vendor, and phone you back with their response. The vendor may wish to reflect upon your offer for a couple of days, discuss it with their spouse, or see if another buyer comes up with a better offer, before making their decision.

Most vendors need to achieve a certain price on their property in order to be able to afford their next one. Do not be unnerved if you do not hear anything from the estate agent for a couple of days, and resist the temptation of calling them to chase up an answer. The estate agent is acting in the interests of the vendor, and if they sense that you are keen on a property, they will advise the vendor to hold out for more money.

If your offer is rejected

It is very unlikely that the vendor will accept your first offer. But unless you make a ridiculously low offer, they are equally unlikely to dismiss it outright, unless of course they receive a higher offer in the interim. If your initial offer is rejected, but you are still keen on the property, decide on a ceiling price and increase your offer in small increments. The estate agent will put pressure on you to increase your bid by saying they have a string of other buyers who are very interested in the property, but stick to your guns and keep your cool. If you are an organised buyer, the vendor is likely to meet you halfway eventually.

When your offer is accepted

Hearing that your offer on your dream home has been accepted is joyous news. However, there is still an awful lot of work to be done before you can exchange contracts and be certain that the home will be yours.

The first thing you need to do is inform your solicitor or conveyancer, so that they can begin to gather all the paperwork necessary to complete the purchase and to transfer ownership of the property from the vendor to you. Completing all the legal work involves a great deal of paper shuffling, and is the most time-consuming and stressful part of buying a property.

As I have said, once the new Home Information Packs come into force, you will have much of the information you are about to collate at your fingertips when you make your offer, and should therefore be able to skip the next two sections and exchange contracts pretty much immediately.

7 Get a survey done

One of the most important stages in buying a property is getting a survey done. A survey is a bit like a health examination of your potential home – it alerts you to defects in the fabric of the property such as a leaky roof, dry rot, condensation, poor insulation, unsafe boilers or ancient fuse boxes, all of which could cost several thousands of pounds to put right, and might even sway your decision as to whether or not to go ahead with the purchase.

Until you have seen a survey report of the property, you do not really know what you are buying – and yet a whopping 80 per cent of homebuyers go ahead and buy homes worth hundreds of thousands of pounds without obtaining a survey first. This is financial madness. If there is a serious defect in the property that you are not aware of, it could not only end up costing you several thousands of pounds in years to come, but could also make it very difficult for you to sell the property later, particularly once the new Home Information Packs come into force. You wouldn't buy a second-hand car from a dealer who couldn't produce a full service history, so don't even think about buying a property without getting a survey done.

The valuation
The first 'survey' that will be carried out on the property is likely to be the mortgage lender's valuation survey. All mortgage lenders will carry out (and usually ask you to pay

for) a *valuation survey* before advancing you a loan. However, this is not the same as getting your survey done. The valuation is not a thorough investigation of the property, but a quick and basic examination so that the lender can assess whether or not to advance you the money.

While the lender may hold back part of the mortgage if the property requires major structural work, most lenders will not be too worried about rotting windows, dodgy roof tiles and creaking joinery which may cost *you* thousands of pounds to put right, because they *want* to lend you the money.

Homebuyer's survey

As I said above, there are two types of surveys: a homebuyer's survey and a full structural survey. A homebuyer's survey is about ten pages long and follows a standard format. The report will include an assessment of the general condition and value of the property; any signs of movement or cracking due to subsidence; timber defects; signs of damp; an examination of the roof; inspection of the interior; and a non-specialist assessment of services such as gas, electricity, water, heating and drainage.

Full structural survey

If you are buying a very old or unusual property, or your homebuyer's report has uncovered any serious problems, it is advisable to obtain a full structural survey. This is a much more detailed inspection of aspects of the property you may be uncomfortable with, such as damp patches, dodgy plumbing or suspicious cracks. When obtaining a full structural survey, you should put any specific requests you have in writing so that you have something to fall back on if faults appear later. However, bear in mind that surveyors will usually cover themselves by inserting caveats – such as the floorboards or wiring have only been subject to a 'visual inspection'.

If you need to renegotiate your offer

If your mortgage lender decides to hold back part of the mortgage because it has discovered during its valuation survey that major works need to be undertaken, or your survey suggests that you must carry out expensive works, you may want to renegotiate your offer or ask the vendor to carry out the work before you commit to buying the property.

8 Conveyancing

Conveyancing is the fancy term applied to the legal process of transferring ownership of the property from the vendors to the buyers. It is not a difficult job, but it is tedious, which is why in most firms the job is passed on to junior staff, leaving the senior lawyer free to pursue the more glamorous high-court dramas. However, unless you are a qualified legal expert and can afford to spend hours wading through mountains of paperwork, do not attempt to save yourself money by doing the conveyancing yourself. The process is slow and frustrating enough as it is, and if you make a mistake it could end up costing you hundreds of thousands of pounds.

Completing all the necessary investigations in order to prepare the final contract takes time, and it is during this nail-biting process that the purchase of your property is most likely to get held up or fall through. While you and your solicitor are making all the necessary checks on the property you are buying, your vendor will be doing the same for the property they are buying, as well as answering your queries about their own home. If any party discovers anything untoward during this process they are free to pull out of the sale. Sometimes, four or five property sales will collapse just because one buyer or seller in the chain decides to pull out.

With the introduction of the new Home Information Packs, buyers will be provided with all the information they discover at this stage, before making their offer. Of course, this will not prevent chains from being broken, but it should make it a lot less common, as buyers will be able to scrutinise surveys and searches before making an offer, and sellers will not make offers on a property until they know that they have a serious buyer.

Once your solicitor has gathered together all the necessary information and paperwork, they will put together a *draft contract*. It is important that you read and check this thoroughly to ensure that it accurately reflects everything you have agreed verbally with the vendor.

9 Exchange contracts

Once you have exchanged contracts, the sale of the property is legally binding and neither you nor the seller can pull out. The precise moment of exchange will have occurred during a telephone call between your solicitor and the vendor's solicitor. Once your solicitor has informed you that this has happened, you and your vendors will each need to sign a copy of the contract in the presence of a witness. This is the point at which you will also need to hand over your deposit to your solicitor. This is also the stage at which you can relax, for you can be certain that the purchase will go ahead.

The contract

The contract will include: the address of the property, names of the vendor and buyer, the purchase price, and a copy of the entry in the Land Registry to prove ownership of the property. It will also include all the other information gathered during the conveyancing process, such as local authority searches, a pre-printed form detailing the fixtures, fittings, and contents to be included in the sale, and a property information form. This will list answers to any questions you or your solicitor have about the property, such as rights of way, ownership of fences and boundaries, planning consents and building regulation certificates for any works carried out.

Before exchanging contracts, your solicitor will also check that you have the deposit ready and a written mortgage offer, and that the property will be sold with vacant possession. If you are buying a flat, he will also check the terms of the lease. When things are slow, and there is a lot of to-ing and fro-ing between buyers and vendors' solicitors to finalise points in the contract, it can be up to three months after the offer has been agreed before contracts are finally exchanged.

10 Move in!

When you exchange contracts you will also set a completion date, when you can move in. This is usually two weeks after exchange of contracts.

Between exchange and completion

During the few days between exchange of contracts and completion, your solicitor will prepare a transfer document to pass possession of the property from the vendor to yourself, and prepare the final mortgage documents so that the money you have borrowed will be released by electronic transfer at midday on the day of completion. Meanwhile, you should book a removals firm and inform your employer, bank, utilities' companies, schools, family and friends of your change of address.

Completion day

The removal men will arrive bright and early to start packing your possessions and furniture and loading them into the vans. Behind the scenes, your solicitor will be using your mortgage funds to pay the balance of the purchase price of the property to the vendor. The seller's deeds will be handed to your solicitor and any outstanding mortgages they have on the property paid off, and the title deeds passed on to your mortgage lender as security for the loan. The seller usually moves out of the property at midday, and hands over the keys to the estate agent. Once this has happened, you can drive down to the estate agents, pick up the keys, and move into your new home!

Buying in Scotland

The process of buying a home in Scotland is quite different to that in England, Wales and Northern Ireland. Solicitors tend to double up as estate agents, and many properties are sold through solicitors' property centres rather than High Street estate agents. Buyers usually arrange viewings and make offers through solicitors.

Fixed price and upset price

Properties in Scotland are marketed either at a *fixed price* or an *upset price*. If the property is offered at a fixed price, the first buyer to offer that amount secures the home. If the property is marketed at an upset price, this is the lowest price the vendor will accept, and buyers are invited to make offers *above* that price.

If you are interested in buying a property in Scotland, it is imperative that you use a Scottish solicitor. The Law Society of Scotland can provide a list of solicitors in your area if you are unable to find one through recommendation. Once you have found a property you like, you should inform your solicitor, who will then contact the vendor's solicitor to register your interest in the property.

Sealed bids

All offers for property marketed at an upset price are made in the form of *sealed bids*, so you will not know how much competing buyers have offered for the property. You cannot secure a property by offering to pay £100 more than the highest bid, so if you are buying in a popular area there is every chance that you may not secure the first property you make an offer on.

Once you have made an offer on a property in Scotland it is legally binding and you cannot pull out of the sale, as you can in England and Wales, so it vital that you have your finances arranged and conduct a survey immediately. If you lose out on the property to another buyer, you will have lost your survey fees. However, as the Scottish system deters buyers from making arbitrary offers on properties they have no intention of buying, in practice you are unlikely to lose out on several properties.

Negotiation of missives

Six to eight weeks after the offer has been made, your solicitor will send the vendor's solicitor a formal offer, known as a *missive of sale*. As well as stipulating the offer price, this will also include enquiries about the title, the contents to be included in the sale, local searches and a move-in date – typically six to eight weeks after the date of the offer.

Offers for properties in Scotland are usually submitted with a list of pre-conditions the vendor must meet if the offer is accepted. For example, if the survey flags up problems with damp or termites, the vendor must either rectify the problem or compensate the buyer in lieu. This means that there is likely to be a great deal of negotiation between your solicitor and the vendor's solicitor before a satisfactory agreement is reached all around. This process is known as the *'negotiation of missives'*.

Conclusion of missives

Once your offer has been accepted, the sale is completed far quicker than in England and Wales. Your solicitor will send a letter of acceptance to the vendor's solicitor, known as the *'conclusion of missives'*. This is similar to the exchanging of contracts in England and Wales. The sale is legally binding, and both the buyer and seller will be liable for damages if they withdraw.

Completion of the sale

Your solicitor will draw up a new title deed, known as a *disposition,* and conduct any necessary searches. The vendor signs the disposition, and once all the other conditions of the sale have been satisfied, the sale is completed. Unlike buying in England and Wales, you do not put down a deposit, but simply pay the full purchase price on completion. You then receive the new disposition and keys, and the property is yours. Stamp duty of 1 per cent of the purchase price is payable after completion.

Co-ordinating a sale and purchase

There is no doubt that the process of buying a property in Scotland is far more organised than that in England and Wales. Due to the regimented way in which sales and purchases are conducted, there is far less opportunity for gazumping or gazundering (lowering an offer just before contracts are due to be signed), and you will not become stuck in a lengthy chain.

The disadvantage of the system is that it is extremely difficult to co-ordinate a sale and purchase. If you complete all the work on the sale of your property before completing work on the purchase of your next one, you will have to move into temporary accommodation. If you complete work on the purchase of a property before selling your existing one, you may need to take out a bridging loan in order to meet the repayments on both mortgages.

As offers on property in Scotland are legally binding, if you are selling a property in England or Wales, in order to buy a property in Scotland, you would be well advised to complete on the sale of your home down south and move into temporary accommodation while you purchase your next one, rather than make a legally binding offer and find that your own buyer pulls out.

Summary

To make finding and purchasing your dream home as straight-forward and stress-free as possible, follow the property goddess's ten-point plan to securing her dream home.

1) Get prepared:
   a) Work out your timescale: when do you want to move by?
   b) Start gathering information on types of property available in your price range, the pros and cons of different locations, mortgage deals on the market, solicitors and surveyors.
   c) If you have property to sell, what do you need to do to prepare it for the market so you achieve the best possible price?

2) Know what you are looking for in your dream home. Make a long list of all your requirements in terms of:
   a) location
   b) accommodation

Which of these are absolutely essential and which ones are you willing to comprise on?

3) Organise your finances:
   a) Work out how much you can afford to spend on the purchase of the property, including deposit, stamp duty, estate agents fees, surveys and searches, removal costs.

Work out your monthly budget including mortgage, service charges if buying a flat, bills, council tax, parking permits.

b) Find the best mortgage, and keep it under review.

4) Go property shopping:
   a) Use the internet to starting point for finding properties.
   b) Make personal contact with estate agents by telephone or visiting the office.
   c) Make regular calls to agents to let them know you are still looking.

5) Conduct viewings:
   a) First viewing: Does the property appeal? Does it fulfil your essential criteria in terms of location and accommodation?
   b) Second viewing: visit the property at a different time of the day. Scrutinise the exterior, décor, fixtures and fittings more carefully. Is there enough storage space? Will all your furniture fit? What compromises will you have to make to live there? Are they worth it?

6) Put in an offer.
   a) If the property needs major work, obtain estimates from builders, architects, damp specialists;
   b) List all other areas in which you will need to spend money on the property – kitchen, bathroom, general décor;
   c) Deduct these figures from the asking price when you make your offer.
   d) Your first offer is unlikely to be accepted so decide on your ceiling price.

7) Get a survey done:
   a) Obtain a list of local surveyors.
   b) If you are buying an old or unusual property, obtain a full structural survey, if not a homebuyers' report should be sufficient.

8) Conveyancing
   a) Instruct your solicitor as soon as your offer has been accepted.
   b) Put any specific queries you have about the property to him, and pass on the surveyor's report.
   c) Read the vendor's property information form and draft contract carefully to check it includes everything you have agreed verbally.
   d) Have the deposit ready for when you exchange contracts

9) Exchange contracts:
   a) Agree on your completion date when you exchange contracts.
   b) Once you have exchanged contracts, book removal vans and inform utility companies, employers etc of your new address.

10) Move in!
    a) Get a good night's sleep.
    b) Keep important documents such as passport, driving licenses, with you, and put valuables in a safe until you move.
    c) Pack long life milk, tea, coffee, biscuits, cereal, bread, champagne and glasses!
    d) Drive down to the estate agents', pick up the keys and move in!

3

Selling

As we established in Chapter 1, the property goddess always sells her existing home *before* buying her next one. Not only does this ensure that you are 100 per cent ready to buy, it also makes sense from a financial perspective.

Having sold your home you will know exactly how much you have to spend on your next one, rather than just basing your calculations on the asking price. If you exchange contracts on the sale of your home before exchanging contracts on the purchase of your next one, you will also have the deposit money from the buyer sitting in your current account, which will help your cash flow.

In this chapter I will show you how to sell your home as quickly and profitably as possible, through an estate agent or privately. Whichever option you choose, there are three stages to selling a property effectively:

1 Preparing and pricing your home for the market.
2 Marketing your home to find the right buyer.
3 Transferring ownership of the property to the buyer.

Setting a timescale for these things

If you are buying and selling, you should allow *at least six months* between putting your existing home on the market and moving into your next one. To have your property on the market and generating interest in time for the prime house-buying season in early March, you really need to start planning your selling strategy in the New Year. This will give you plenty of time to get rid of clutter, carry out essential repairs and redecoration, and clean and polish your home to give it the 'showcase effect'. It will also give you time to find and instruct a good estate agent, or to draft brochures, take photographs, research where you are going to advertise, and create a webpage, if you intend to sell privately.

1 Preparing and pricing your home for the market

Preparing your home for the market means ensuring that the interior and exterior of the property are in tip-top condition, and that they send out the *right message* to the *right market*, so that you achieve the best possible price. The more effort you put into researching your buyers' market and polishing your property at this stage, the less time you will waste once it is actually up for sale, and the sooner you will be able to move.

Cast your mind back to when you were buying

To sell your property, you need to start looking at it from the buyer's perspective. A good way to start doing this is to cast your mind back to *your* initial impressions of your home when *you* were buying it. It is highly unlikely you thought it was perfect in every way. What reservations did you have about it? What really irked you about it? What changes and improvements have you made, and why?

De-personalise your home

You have lived in your home for several years. You have grown to love (or make do) with its many quirks and features, and made them your own. But prospective buyers are not interested in learning about you, they want to imagine their own lives in the property, so your first job is to thoroughly de-personalise your home. This may not be easy initially, and it is also likely to be exhausting, so you might want to enlist the help of family or friends.

Get rid of personal debris

Start by getting rid of all your personal debris. Take down all the shopping lists, holiday photos and post-it notes from your fridge door; file away bank statements and work appraisals cluttering up the kitchen table; throw away old newspapers and magazines; pick up the roller skates, tennis rackets and half-chewed dog bones from the hallway; and pull out all your old handbags, worn-out shoes and broken appliances stuffed behind, underneath and on top of cupboards and work surfaces.

Sell the dream lifestyle

Next, erase all traces of your idiosyncratic lifestyle – like the metal filing cabinets, laptop and photocopier in the sitting room if you work from home; the exercise bike and rowing machine in the bedroom if you're a fitness fanatic; the tarot cards and crystal balls if you happen to be a psychic! Remember you are selling the 'ideal home' lifestyle.

Store away excess furniture

Take a good look at all the furniture you have in each room, decide which pieces are essential to staging the room to its best advantage, and arrange for everything else to be stored away until you have sold your property.

Display a small selection of ornaments and artefacts

Remove all your ornaments, decorations, paintings, flower vases and pieces of art from the mantelpiece, shelves and walls, lay them all out on the floor, and select a small handful (no more than six objects) that convey a particular theme or mood, and arrange them stylishly in each room. Wrap up all the remaining objects in tissue paper and pack them away into a large cardboard box until you move.

Clean, clean, clean

Having de-cluttered each room, embark on a cleaning mission. Go through your kitchen cupboards, fridge and bathroom cabinets, and throw away all food, condiments, bath gels and shampoos, medicines, etc. past their sell-by dates (buyers are nosy people). Get the carpets, curtains and windows professionally cleaned, and scrub the oven, kitchen floor and bathroom fittings until they sparkle.

Make a list of all minor repairs that need doing

Buyers notice the tiniest things, so before calling in the estate agents, attend to all the minor jobs you've been putting off. Walk around each room examining the walls, floors and ceilings carefully, and make a note of all the cracks, damp patches, peeling paint, loose handles and broken hinges.

Failing to attend to these makes your home look unloved, and is a careless way of losing buyers, so put aside as many weekends as necessary to get the property immaculate.

If the walls are looking a bit grubby, freshen them up with a few coats of fashionably-coloured paint. Smarten up old kitchen units and doors with new handles, and invest in some elegant dimmer switches to create more intimate lighting in the sitting room and bedrooms. By the time your property is ready to go on the market, you should be feeling slightly envious of the new owners!

Major repairs

Most vendors do not have an unlimited budget to spruce up their home for the market, so if your property requires major works such as new windows, a new roof, gas central heating or new wiring, consult a local estate agent to see whether it is actually worth getting this work done yourself, or accepting a slightly lower offer from a buyer in lieu.

In popular locations where demand for property is high, carrying out such major repairs might be 'negative benefits' as buyers will not know what the property was like before. If, once the property is on the market, you discover that the rotting windows and missing roof tiles are keeping buyers away, then you will either have to dig deep into your pockets to put them right, or drop the price.

Tidy up every day

Once your property is on the market, get into the habit of emptying all the bins and generally tidying up, every day. Avoid cooking smelly foods just before viewings, always have fresh flowers and scented candles in the home, and if you have pets, keep them well out of the way.

Market research

If you were applying for a plum job, you would research the company and what makes it tick, and make yourself stand out from the other applicants. Similarly, to achieve a quick and profitable house sale, you need to understand what prospective buyers want, and put your home ahead of the competition.

What sector of the buying market are you selling to? First-time buyers, affluent young professionals, young families, retired couples? Are they smart media types who go for minimalist contemporary décor, or suburbanites who go for more traditional period fare? Do they eat out several times a week and only use the kitchen for heating up fancy microwave meals, or do they need a spacious kitchen to prepare kids' teas and family suppers? Do they prefer patios or lawns?

Give your home an edge over the competition

How do other properties up for sale in the area compare to yours in terms of: the number of bedrooms and bathrooms, layout, décor, quality of fixtures and fittings, outdoor space, parking facilities and general condition? What can you do to your property to give it an edge over the competition? It could be something as simple as new bedroom lighting, or creating a stylish focal point in the sitting room, but it might just clinch the deal.

Is it a buyers' or sellers' market?

You should also quiz local estate agents on the current state of the market. If there are numerous properties in immaculate condition, you are competing in a buyers' market and will have to go the extra mile to give your property the 'wow' factor. If there are dozens of buyers chasing one or two properties, you are in a sellers' market and can relax a little.

Find out what sells and what sticks

Find out what prices have been achieved for similar properties in the area in the past three months, and how long it took to sell them. If a particular property was slow to sell, what made it stick for so long? What improvements did the vendors make before eventually finding a buyer? If a certain property literally sold overnight, what really clinched the deal? Establishing this sort of information *before* you put your property on the market will give you a head start, and save you months of grief and frustration once the 'For Sale' boards go up.

Give your home a top-to-toe makeover

Kerbstone appeal

Rather than waste precious time viewing dozens of lousy properties they wouldn't dream of living in, many buyers will spend a couple of hours on a Sunday afternoon driving by ten or fifteen homes on the market and only arranging viewings for the ones that look promising from the outside. Don't lose them at this stage. Dustbins overflowing with rubbish, grubby windows, missing roof tiles and broken drainpipes will have them revving the accelerator and driving off to the next property on their list without giving yours a backward glance. So before you start working on the inside of the property, make sure that the outside looks a million dollars.

Four ways to give your property kerbstone appeal:

- Paint the front door blue (research shows that for some reason a blue front door appeals strongly to buyers). Make sure it has a number plaque – buyers get very frustrated when they can't find a property. (Also, for viewings, make sure there is a doorbell that works, and that can be heard upstairs and from the back of the garden – pressing a bell that doesn't ring or can't be heard is very disconcerting.)

- Get all the windows professionally cleaned so that they *sparkle*. Buy some windowboxes and fill them with pretty seasonal flowers. Keep them well trimmed and watered.
- Sweep away litter, leaves and other debris from the driveway on a daily basis. Get rid of black dustbins, recycling boxes and empty milk bottles, and invest in some colourful potted shrubs or perennials.
- Fit a sensor-controlled outdoor light so visitors after dark feel more secure when walking up the driveway. A burglar alarm will also reassure buyers that you are a security-conscious homeowner.

The front room, or other rooms seen from the outside

As well as scrutinising the exterior of the property, drive-by buyers also form conclusions about vendors by peering into their front windows. Net curtains, bicycles, storage boxes and computers scream 'bedsitter land', and should be replaced with deep sofas, table lamps, and coffee tables scattered with illustrated books.

The interior

More than ever today, when selling a home you are selling an aspirational lifestyle. Most buyers lack imagination (and patience), so as a vendor you need to present the lifestyle on a plate. To do this, ensure that each room suggests that it is used for a specific purpose: sleeping, eating and entertaining, relaxing, and that it has a focal point.

The hall

Buyers usually make up their minds about a property within thirty seconds of entering it. The hallway is the first area they will see, so it is imperative that it is bright, clean and welcoming. Get rid of briefcases, kids' tricycles, coats and shoes. A mirror will make the entrance hall look lighter and more spacious. If you have room in the hall, a small table with a beautiful lamp or vase of flowers will create a stylish entrance.

Living room

The living room is the place we go to relax and unwind at the end of a hard day, and where we entertain family and friends, so it should be tasteful, restful and elegant. In a period property, the focal point of the sitting room is usually the fireplace, so draw attention to it by hanging a large mirror above the mantelpiece. Arrange deep sofas and perhaps a couple of small armchairs or large cushions around a low coffee table, but be careful not to make the room look too cluttered. If your sofas are a bit worn, cover them with luxurious throws and cushions. Remove all your photos, mail and party invitations from the mantelpiece and shelves, and replace them with colour co-ordinated flower vases, candles and lots of good books.

Kitchen

As I said in Chapter 2, the kitchen is the most expensive room in the house to replace, and can make or break a sale. It is also the one room where you really must know your buyers' market. Affluent young professionals will demand sleek and contemporary units, microwaves, fridges and dishwashers. They will also want entertaining space, so if the kitchen is large enough, put in a dining table and chairs, and dress them with stylish dinner party ware, flowers and candles.

For families, the kitchen is usually a multi-purpose room where they have family suppers, where the kids do their homework, and where friends congregate for informal coffees and chats, so if you are selling to this market, go for a more homely style. Trends in kitchen designs change rapidly, so whatever bracket your home falls into, don't go for anything too cutting edge or it will look dated by the end of the year.

Again, clear away all your clutter from the floors, cupboards and work surfaces, and display a few nice bottles of flavoured oils, pastas, herbs and jams.

Main bedroom

The focal point of the master bedroom should obviously be a sumptuously made bed, and there should be bedside tables with reading lights at each side of the bed. Large, well-organised wardrobes are much appreciated by women buyers. If you are lucky enough to have one, tidy up your shoes and bags, and hang up skirts and trousers, to show the wardrobe off to its best advantage.

Bathroom

Gone are the days when retro-style avocado and tangerine-coloured bathroom suites were the height of fashion. Bathrooms suites today *must* be white. They must also be totally spotless, so scrub every last trace of limescale from the taps, sink and bath, and clean the grouting between the tiles. Invest in a good power shower and have a stock of clean shower curtains and bath mats. If you are selling a Victorian property and have a large bathroom, consider investing in a stylish freestanding claw-foot bath; it will add elegance and create a focal point.

Replace the radiator with a smart heated towel rail, and under no circumstances carpet the bathroom floor – it will get wet and start to smell. Throw away half-filled shampoo bottles, face-wash and unwanted Christmas presents, and replace them with a few elegant top-of-the-range products and piles of thick, fluffy white towels.

Create harmony

Each room may be decorated differently, but overall the décor should be harmonious and consistent, otherwise the property will feel disjointed. A quick and effective way of creating harmony in a home is to introduce a recurring colour theme throughout. So if you buy some smart raspberry- and cream-coloured storage boxes for the sitting room, dot a few raspberry-coloured mugs and cream candles in the kitchen, put some raspberry-coloured hand towels in the bathroom, and cover the bed with a cream bedspread with a raspberry-coloured trim.

Gardens and sheds

A neglected garden is not a pleasant sight, and will give buyers more ammunition to bargain over the asking price. If you are a keen gardener and have cultivated beautiful lawns and borders, it can add several thousands of pounds to the price of your property. But don't fork out money on fancy landscaping if you haven't got a 'designer garden'. Most buyers do not appreciate gardens that are too high maintenance, and a professionally manicured lawn is unlikely to add a penny to the value of your property. A quick tidy up and some cheap garden furniture will do.

Quick fixes for neglected gardens:

- Mow the lawn, trim the edges, and get rid of weeds.
- Clear away all household and garden rubbish you may have dumped in the garden.
- Mend broken fences, and consider giving worn-looking ones a lick of paint.
- Fix hanging baskets filled with lavender at nose level, next to the back door.
- Dot the patio with cheap colourful plants like geraniums and impatiens, and put out some cheap garden tables and chairs.

Pricing your property

Having given your home the top-to-toe 'house doctor' treatment, you need to decide on your selling price.

Estate agents' valuations

Invite at least three local estate agents to give you a valuation, but don't expect the accuracy of rocket science. You are likely to find that agents' valuations vary wildly for no particular reason. This is because, unlike surveyors, estate agents are not duty-bound to examine the size and condition of a property when giving a valuation. Most will simply compare them to similar properties for sale in the area and then make an educated guess.

This is why it is important to obtain at least three valuations, and to use your own judgment, backed up by your own market sense. If there is a huge difference between the highest and lowest valuations, ask the agents to back up their quotes and opt for something slightly above the middle price. If you market the property too cheaply, you will rob yourself of several thousands of pounds, but if you over-price it, you risk alienating buyers altogether and not getting any viewings.

Make the price attractive

Whatever price you decide on, make sure that the figure looks attractive. If your property is worth £250,000, price it at £249,950 – it is only a difference of £50, but psychologically a buyer will automatically perceive it to be better value. Also, bear in mind the stamp duty brackets. A £260,000 home will cost a buyer £5,400 more in stamp duty than one priced at £240,000 – and a £525,000 property would cost a cool £11,550 more than a £490,000 one!

2 Marketing your home to find the right buyer

Having prepared your property for the market and given it a price, you need to market it and secure a reliable buyer. As mentioned previously, you can either do this through an estate agent, or privately.

How to find an estate agent

If you decide to use an estate agent, it is important that you choose one with whom you can develop a good rapport. Your estate agent's main job is to find the right buyer and secure the best possible price for the property. However, a good agent will also be able to advise you on presentation if the property is not generating interest and, more crucially, work hard to keep the chain intact if things start going pear-shaped once you have accepted an offer.

Seven steps to finding a good estate agent:

- *Qualifications*: There is nothing to stop an unqualified estate agent from setting up a business, and problems usually occur when an unwitting vendor resorts to using one, so check the estate agent's credentials. They should have one or all of the following qualifications: ARICS (Associate of Royal Institute of Chartered Surveyors), ANAEA (Associate of the National Association of Estate Agents), or ASVA (Associate of the Society of Valuers and Auctioneers).
- *Fees*: You can expect the agent to quote a commission fee of between 1.5 per cent and 2.5 per cent of the eventual sale price for sole representation, and up to 3 per cent of the sale price if you choose to market the property with several agents. The actual percentage will depend on how much work the agent thinks they will have to do in order to secure a sale. If you have done your homework and

believe your property will be easy to sell, you should be able to negotiate a lower percentage.

- *Marketing*: The fee should include all the costs of marketing the property such as colour photographs and classified adverts. Ask the agent if they will include a floor plan of the property in the particulars. Examine the particulars of other properties they are selling. Do they look attractive? Are the details presented logically? Do they sound accurate? Ask the agent if your property will be advertised in their office window and/or in local newspapers? Does the agency have an up-to-date website? If they are a nationwide chain, will they advertise your property in other branches? Also, ask them about their opening hours – busy professionals are more likely to go househunting late in the evening or at weekends. And think about the physical location of the estate agent's office. Buyers are lazy, and an estate agent's office located right next to the station or in the centre of town is likely to receive far more custom than one tucked away out of sight.

- *Viewings*: Will the agent accompany the buyers on viewings or will they expect you to show them around the property yourself? Do they treat buyers with the same courtesy and respect as they do the sellers who are paying them?

- *Passing on offers*: Your estate agent should make your property available to all serious buyers, and pass on all offers to you. Once you have accepted an offer you should instruct the agent to take the property off the market, as keeping it on just in case another buyer comes along with a higher offer is dishonourable. Unfortunately, there are some unscrupulous agents around, who will undervalue your property, get a friend to buy it, and then sell it on for a vast profit. Others have also been known to accept a bribe from the buyer in order to 'reserve' the property, or to ring-fence the property so they can sell it to friends or family. If your property is not generating interest within a couple of weeks, or the first and only buyer to view the property makes you an offer almost immediately, you may have cause to become suspicious.

- *Vetting the buyers*: Your estate agent should vet the buyers who put forward offers to ensure that they are serious purchasers and not timewasters. If they are first-time buyers, have they got their mortgage arranged and deposit ready? If the buyer has property to sell, is it on the market and generating interest from other buyers?

- *Holding your hand until completion*: If the sale of your property is one in a long chain of transactions, things can become very stressful if one of the sales in the chain falls through. This is where a good estate agent can be worth his weight in gold. An experienced agent will use his negotiating skills to try to keep the chain together, by chivvying everyone along and encouraging them to exchange on time, while a lousy one will simply move on to the next instruction and leave you high and dry, once they have found you a buyer.

Issuing instructions to sell

Once you have found an agent you need to issue them with instructions to sell. They will confirm their fees in writing, and spell out how long you are tied to them before you can instruct another agent. This period should be no more than six weeks, as if your property is not generating considerable interest by then, it will require a fresh approach.

The particulars

Having received instructions to sell, your agent will draw up the particulars for your property. Agents will be dealing with several properties at once, so check that the details are correct and that no important features have been left out.

Viewings

If the estate agent accompanies the buyer on viewings, it is best to stay out of the way, as buyers tend to feel intimidated if vendors are breathing down their necks. If you are conducting viewings yourself, be courteous and businesslike rather than overly friendly and chatty. Give buyers a running commentary of the property as you show them around, but do not overload them with information, or point out too many features at once. Have a plan in mind, but conduct the viewing at their pace. Buyers will ask why you are moving. Be careful how you answer. If you are five months' pregnant and selling a one-bedroom flat, they will twig that you need to move quickly and might well be tempted to try their luck by making a low offer.

If you are not receiving offers within four weeks

It is only human nature for estate agents to direct most of their energies into properties that are easy to sell – after all, that is how they earn their living. If you are not receiving serious offers within four weeks of putting your home on the market, ask the agent why they think the property might be sticking. Then, put the problem right and market the property again. If you feel your old estate agent has lost enthusiasm, move to another one, but be wary of changing agents too many times. Buyers have sharp eyes, and will become suspicious of a home that is constantly being 'rebranded'.

Sole agent or multiple agents?

If you decide to market your property with more than one agent, it will cost you a lot more in commission as the agents will be working in competition with one another. Unless you are really desperate for a quick sale, it isn't worth spending the extra money to have your property listed in several agents' books. Serious buyers will register with several agents in the area anyway.

Accepting an offer

Unless your property is truly exceptional and you are operating in a real sellers' market in which properties are being snapped up the day they come on to the market, be wary of a buyer who offers the full asking price in the first round of negotiations. There are many unscrupulous buyers who will go around making offers on several properties simply to 'reserve' them while they carry on looking. Others will put in offers just to test the market and see what they can get away with. Shrewd agents should know their buyers as well as their sellers and be able to separate the genuine purchasers from the timewasters.

Setting your floor price

When you put your property on the market, you also should decide on your floor price – that is, the minimum price at which you are prepared to sell the property. Most vendors set a floor of 3 per cent to 5 per cent below the asking price. So, if your property is on the market for £250,000, you should expect to achieve £237,500–£242,500. If you receive an offer that is 10–15 per cent below your asking price from a serious buyer, encourage them to increase their bid until they come up with a more acceptable offer, but do not haggle to death. It will create bad feeling, and the buyers may drag their feet in the run up to exchanging contracts.

How to sell your home yourself

As we have seen, instructing an estate agent is rather an expensive way of finding a buyer, and the growth of property websites has made it much easier to sell your home privately. But this is not an option for the faint-hearted. Do not underestimate the amount of work that will be involved in doing all the marketing and negotiating yourself, nor the number of buyers who will mess you around by failing to turn up to viewings, or simply arrange viewings because they fancy having a look inside your home.

Selling your home yourself will be considerably cheaper than using an agent, but it won't be free. Before taking the plunge, tot up the cost of producing colour photos and brochures, placing adverts in newspapers and on websites, as well as the time you will have to devote to responding to queries, chasing up buyers for feedback, and negotiating the sale through to completion, before deciding whether it really is for you.

Photos

The first thing you will need to do is to take some good colour photos of your property. Ideally, you should have a photo of the outside of the property, and a handful of photos of the interior. Most buyers decide whether or not to view a property on the basis of the photos, so take pictures of the rooms that really sell a lifestyle, such as the newly fitted kitchen with a lovely entertaining space, or the cosy sitting room with a Victorian fireplace.

Producing a brochure

Before starting to draft your brochure, make a list of all the features that you need to include, such as walk-in wardrobes, double sinks in the kitchen, period fireplaces and built-in shelving in the sitting room. Present the information in the order that the buyers will view the property, and ask a friend to check it all. Producing a top-notch brochure might well take a couple of drafts, so don't be too hasty to start printing!

Placing a classified advert

Having drafted the brochure, you need to produce an attention-grabbing advert to place in the classified sections of local newspapers. This should be short, snappy and include:

the style of property you are selling (e.g. Victorian conversion flat, modern terraced house) and its location; the number of bedrooms and bathrooms; other rooms in the house; gardens and garages; striking features and décor; and of course the price. Play around with the wording until you come up with something really eye-catching.

Most papers will require copy at least a week before publication, but if you miss the deadline or they have too many adverts for that week, yours might be held over till the next week. Buyers usually scan the papers the day they come out, so it is crucial that you know when your advert will appear and that you are 100 per cent ready to take their calls, or otherwise it will all be a waste of time.

Creating a webpage

The internet has revolutionised the property industry, and there are now more than fifty websites where you can advertise your property. The most basic sites charge about £50 to display a few photos and a brief description of the property. The most sophisticated ones can cost more than £300 and include a 'video tour' of your property, digital photos, floor plans, and a 'For Sale' board.

Searching for a home is tiring and time-consuming, and there is nothing buyers love more than a bit of armchair browsing, so it is well worth splashing out on a really attractive online advert, even if you are using an estate agent.

Weeding out unsuitable 'buyers'

As a private seller, as well as scrutinising prospective buyers' ability to go through with the purchase, you should also be mindful of security, particularly if you are a single woman. Do not disclose your full address, name or home telephone number on your webpage – a first name and mobile number is sufficient.

Set up a dedicated e-mail address. If buyers e-mail you with questions about the property, or to arrange a viewing, request a telephone number on which you can call them back. Ask them a few basic questions such as how long they have been looking in the area, and whether they have a property to sell themselves – this should establish whether they are genuine or not. Before letting them into your property, obtain their full name, home address and telephone number.

If a speculative buyer knocks on your door requesting a viewing, take their name, address and phone number and tell them that you will call them back to arrange a more convenient time to show them around.

3 Transferring ownership of the property to the buyer

Once you have accepted an offer, you need to inform your solicitor of the buyer's details, so that he can prepare a standard property information form and a draft contract. As I have said, under the current system, the period between accepting an offer and exchanging contracts is the most stressful and nail-biting of all, as the buyer can decide to pull out at any stage. For this reason, you should not take the property off the market until you are satisfied that your purchaser really is 100 per cent ready to buy.

The survey and valuation

A serious buyer will quickly commission a survey or mortgage valuation. If you have not heard from their surveyor within two weeks of accepting their offer, call your estate agent to find out what's going on. Is the surveyor simply overworked or being inefficient, or is the buyer having second thoughts or running into problems getting a mortgage? If it is the latter, inform them that you will put the property back on the market if they do not receive a call from their surveyor/mortgage lender within the next two weeks.

First impressions count with surveyors as well as buyers, so once again tidy up. If you have had any major repairs carried out on the property such as a new roof, windows or damp-proof courses, leave a copy of the relevant warranties on the kitchen table for them to inspect.

No property is perfect, and as a general rule surveys make quite depressing reading. If the buyer's lender or surveyor down-values the property and your buyer uses this as an excuse to renegotiate the price, ask to see a copy of the survey. If it simply 'recommends' that the buyer carries out certain improvements, the problems are unlikely to be that serious, and you should not give in to 'gazundering'.

The draft contract

While your buyer is getting surveys and valuations carried out, your solicitor will be contacting your mortgage lender to request the title deeds to the property. They will also send you a property information form, which you are obliged to complete honestly. If you do not know the answer to a question such as 'who owns the boundaries?', write 'don't know' rather than give a false answer. You should also provide your solicitor with copies of warranties, guarantees and planning permission certificates. Once your solicitor has gathered all this information, he will put together a draft contract for your buyer to peruse.

Your buyer is likely to come back with questions or request amendments to the contract. However, you are only obliged to answer those pertaining to ownership of the land. If the buyer has questions regarding the structural state of the property, ask them to put the queries to their own surveyor. The buyer will hold you to all statements you make, and it is dangerous for you to pass comment on the structural condition of the property if you are not a qualified expert. As I said, once the new Home Information Packs come into force, you will have to provide your buyer with a survey, local authority searches, title deeds – and copies of the lease and service charges if you are buying a flat – at the viewing stage, so they should be able to exchange contracts much quicker.

Once the buyer is satisfied that they have made all the necessary checks, their solicitor calls your solicitor to say that they are ready to exchange contracts.

Exchanging contracts

Selling a property requires considerably less legal work on your behalf than buying one, as it is the buyer's solicitor who makes all the checks and undertakes all the searches. But you should read the contract carefully to check that it contains all agreed alterations, and none that have not been agreed. As I said, once you have exchanged contracts you are legally obliged to sell. When you exchange contracts, your buyer will also hand over their deposit. If you have used an estate agent to find a buyer, you should inform them that you have exchanged contracts, and settle the fee now.

Completion day

Your solicitor will call to say he has received the balance of the purchase price from the buyer's solicitor, and pass on the title deeds and any other documentation relating to the house in return. The financial transaction usually happens around mid-morning. The property now belongs to your buyer and you should prepare to move out and hand over the keys to the estate agent if you have used one, or directly to the buyer if you have not.

Summary

The property goddess always sells her existing home before buying her next one, and allows at least six months between putting her home on the market and moving into her new one.

1) Prepare your home for the market:
   a) Start looking at your home from a buyer's perspective. Attend to minor repairs, de-personalise the property, get rid of clutter, store away excess furniture and clean, clean, clean from top to bottom. Once your home is on the market, tidy up every day.
   b) Stage your house to give it the showhome effect. Create a focal point in each room. Use ornaments, mirrors, soft furnishings and lighting to give each room the 'wow factor'. Each room may be decorated differently, but the property should feel harmonious overall.

2) Put the property on the market:
   a) Invite at least three agents to provide you with a valuation.
   b) Make the price attractive. Bear in mind the stamp duty brackets.
   c) Instruct an agent, or market the property yourself.

3) Find a buyer:
   a) Keep a record of all viewings.
   b) Do not accept an offer from a first-time buyer who has not arranged their finances, or a buyer whose property is not yet under offer.

4) Transferring ownership of the property:
   a) Answer all questions on the property information form

honestly, but do not make statements about the structure of the property.

b) Read the draft contract carefully to ensure it does not contain anything you have not agreed.

c) On completion day, it is courteous to leave the property clean and tidy.

4

Adding Value

Once you have bought your home, every change you make to the exterior, the structure and size of the property, and the fixtures, fittings and décor, will affect its value to a greater or a lesser degree when you come to sell. As I said in Chapter 1, there is a big difference between making strategic improvements that will add real value to your home and simply 'doing it up'. Before carrying out a major project, ask yourself: will this change significantly enhance my quality of life, and that of future occupants, or is it just a cosmetic improvement?

Buyers will always pay more for homes with bright loft conversions that will make great study-bedrooms for their teenage children; open-plan kitchens that offer fluid cooking, eating and entertaining spaces; extra guest bedrooms; and en-suite bathrooms. But ritzy marble floor tiles imported from Italy, hand-made study-room furniture, and Dallas-style jacuzzis and gyms in the bedrooms will not ease pressure off the main bathroom in the morning rush hour, or provide extra space to accommodate friends and family at Christmas. At best they'll be seen as gimmicky – and at worst they'll make your home look like a stage-set for an episode of *Footballers' Wives*!

The top seven home improvements almost guaranteed to add value to properties are: gas central heating, double-glazing, new kitchens and bathrooms, extensions, loft conversions and garages. In this chapter, I will explain how to organise such improvements, comply with building regulations, obtain planning permission, and find good architects and builders. I will also provide some basic tips on routine home maintenance, such as avoiding burst pipes, damp and condensation, and how to get the best results when decorating.

Financing home improvements

Before undertaking any home improvements, work out a budget for materials and labour costs, and factor in at least an *extra 10 per cent for unexpected extras.* If you are carrying out substantial works or renovating an entire property and need to borrow money, either take out a cheap personal loan, or borrow extra on your mortgage.

The latter option is recommended if you need to borrow a significant amount (over £20,000), but be sure that you will be able to meet the higher repayments now, and also if interest rates rise by a couple of per cent, before committing yourself. In addition, add on the cost of any arrangement and valuation fees that your lender will levy.

If you are planning to re-mortgage, you might want to consider a flexible mortgage. This will allow you to borrow extra funds above the value of your mortgage, up to a certain limit. So, if your existing mortgage is £95,000 and your property is worth £230,000, you could take out a flexible mortgage with a limit of £125,000, which would allow you to withdraw £30,000. Credit cards and overdrafts are the most expensive form of borrowing and are not recommended for financing large, long-term home improvements.

Gas central heating

Of all home improvements, gas central heating is the one that will add most value to a property, so if you currently have electric heating in your home, make installing a gas boiler and radiators your top priority. It will cost about £5,000 to install, but you should recoup 80 per cent of the cost when you move.

Gas boilers may only be fitted by professional installers registered by the Council of Registered Gas Installers (CORGI) and, once installed, should be serviced once a year. There are two main types of boilers: *traditional boilers* and *combination boilers*.

A traditional boiler heats water in a similar way to a gas burner under a kettle. It operates quietly and efficiently, and has reliable controls that are easy to understand. Although traditional boilers consume a relatively large amount of fuel, this is offset by the boiler's reliability. Traditional boilers can be used with fully pumped or gravity-driven hot water systems. They come in a huge range of sizes, and are therefore suitable for all types of property, from terraced houses to mansions.

Combination boilers provide hot water for the central heating system and instant hot water for the taps. The water for the central heating is heated in a closed circuit like any other boiler, but the water for the hot taps is fed from the mains through the boiler and then directly to the taps, rather than being stored in a hot-water cylinder, as with a traditional boiler. Combination boilers are suitable for small flats and houses, as the lack of a tank saves space, but are not recommended in larger properties where several people may require hot water at the same time. The internal workings of combination boilers are complicated and they can be expensive to repair, so it is a good idea to take out a maintenance contract.

Adding space

There is a growing trend among homeowners who require more living space to expand their properties through loft conversions, side and back extensions, and conservatories, rather than uproot themselves and move to a larger home. And in many cases this makes a lot of sense, both financially and practically.

As we have seen, moving from a two-bedroom house worth £240,000 to a larger three-bedroom one worth £300,000 would cost £9,000 in stamp duty, at least £5,000 in estate agents' and legal fees, plus the larger repayments on a bigger mortgage. On top of this, there would be the stress of selling the home and finding another one, moving and settling in.

So if you have a large loft space that can be converted into a bright, airy bedroom with an en-suite bathroom for £20,000, you might well conclude that this is the better option. As well as being less disruptive, it will also be a lot quicker. Finding and moving into a new home can take several months, but a loft conversion can usually be completed in four to six weeks, once planning permission has been granted.

Extensions

Extending the exterior walls to the side or back of the property is a great way of adding more space and light to a home. A good architect can often come up with a plan to transform a small, dark room with awkward proportions into a fabulously light, fluid and contemporary living space, which can greatly enhance your quality of life and add thousands of pounds to the value of a property.

But before thinking of building an extension, make sure that:

- You do actually have space to extend into, without ruining the style of the property.
- You will not be over-expanding your home. If your property already provides maximum accommodation for its size in relation to other properties in your street, expanding it further is more likely to detract rather than add value.
- The extension will not upset the overall balance of the property by making it too top-heavy or elongated.

Planning permission

The figures and restrictions that define whether or not you will require planning permission to carry out an extension are confusing, and will depend a) on the size of the project, and b) whether or not the property has been extended before.

Regulations are also subject to change and can differ from one area to another, so before drawing up plans it is best to consult a qualified surveyor or architect who is conversant with the prevailing building and planning regulations in your local area. As a general rule, provided your property is not a listed building or located in a conservation area, it can be enlarged by up to 15 per cent of the volume of the original house. Terraced houses can be expanded by up to 10 per cent of their volume.

Under no circumstances be tempted to begin work on an extension before obtaining planning permission. Although some local authorities will grant certificates retrospectively, this is by no means guaranteed, and if permission is not granted you may have to pull down the work and return the property to its original condition.

Conservatories

Building a conservatory is an economical way of adding more light and living space to a property, and experts reckon that in the right area you could recoup 40 per cent of the cost when you come to sell.

Conservatories come in a great many shapes and sizes – the smallest ones almost resemble greenhouses, while the largest ones can accommodate a swimming pool.

When choosing a conservatory, be careful to select a style that will suit your property in terms of design and proportion. Engaging an architect to design a conservatory specifically for your property will be more expensive than buying a ready-made one from a double-glazing company or DIY superstore, but will look more stylish as well as allowing you to design the room for your own needs. Although conservatories trap heat from the sun even on the most overcast days, they will still require adequate heating for the winter months, and good ventilation and heat-reflecting glass or blinds for the summer.

Lofts

Loft conversions are generally easier to build and will cause less disruption to the household than an extension, as the structure and foundations will already be in place. There is no more digging required, so the sky is the limit. But before contacting an architect to come up with a grand design for your loft space, check that it is suitable for conversion.

For the loft space to be used as a bedroom or living area, it must have minimum head clearance of 2.3 metres; if it does not, it can only be used as a storage space. In most properties, the first floor ceiling joists are unlikely to be strong enough to bear the weight of furniture and occupants, and will need strengthening with extra beams. Most properties will also require extra support around the rafters for the windows.

As well as checking the height of the loft ceiling, check that the landing space on the first floor is large enough to accommodate a staircase. Pull-down ladders are not practical for lofts that will be used on a day-to-day basis, and will not add value to your property.

Planning permission and building regulations relating to lofts

If your loft conversion includes a dormer window it is more than likely to require planning permission. Large dormer loft extensions are usually only permitted at the back of the property.

Regardless of whether or not the conversion requires planning permission, the plan will need to be vetted by your local authority and the work inspected by a building controls' inspector. The windows must provide a suitable fire escape and be accessible by ladder from the ground outside.

The staircase

In smaller properties where the landing area is restricted, finding the space to build a new staircase for a loft conversion can be a problem. There are two main ways of overcoming this: you can create more space by moving an internal wall in one of the bedrooms, or build a spiral or turning staircase. A staircase with one 90 degree turn is known as a single winder, a staircase with two turns is known as a double winder. All loft conversions must have a rooflight or dormer window that is large enough to provide an escape in the event of a fire, and be accessible from the ground by a ladder.

Plumbing

If your water tank is situated in the loft, you can either leave that part of the loft unconverted, or create a ceiling in the new loft room and accommodate the tank there. If the new loft incorporates an en-suite bathroom, you may need to fit a pump to the tank to create a sufficient head of pressure for the water to flow adequately.

Furniture and storage space

Although the furniture and furnishings are usually the last items to be fitted into a loft room, they should be planned well in advance as they may have to be transported up a narrow or steep staircase. Avoid buying large sofabeds with heavy built-in bed frames. Make the most of all the eaves in the room by incorporating built-in storage cupboards into the design. Only buy flat-packed wardrobes.

Finding professionals when creating extra space

The growth in the number of homeowners carrying out extensions, loft conversions and home improvements is putting pressure on the construction industry, and allowing rogue builders and cowboy architects to cash in on the shortage of qualified professionals. In 2003, the Trading Standards' Agency received more than 100,000 complaints against rogue builders and tradesmen. But while horror stories abound, if you source and vet prospective builders and architects thoroughly before allowing them into your home and parting with your cash, you should end up with professional results that give you years of pleasure and also add value to your home.

Using an architect

Today's typical British homeowner wants to live in a home that looks and feels Victorian, Georgian or Edwardian from the outside, but offers light, fluid accommodation that is suitable for busy, multi-task contemporary lifestyles on the inside. This is where an experienced architect, with vision and imagination, can work wonders.

By opening up hallways, removing doorways, shifting corridors, repositioning partition walls and extending external ones, adding windows and rooflights, a good architect can transform a small, dark room with awkward period proportions into a stunning modern space that will improve the way you feel about your home, make day-to-day living easier and more enjoyable, and add value to the property. But remember, once the work has been done it is likely to be irrevocable and you will be stuck with the changes, so take time to find the right architect and design.

Finding your dream architect

Invite three architects to come up with designs, plans and costings. Most architects will charge between £80 and £100 an hour for a consultation. Since 1997, the Royal Institute of British Architects (RIBA) has been running an annual Architect in the House scheme, during which you can receive an hour-long consultation with a member architect, with no obligation to act on their plans or advice, in return for a minimum donation of £20, which goes to the charity Shelter.

Design solutions

Explain to your architect all the compromises you have had to make while living in your home, and how you hope these things can be improved. Mention any specific changes or improvements you would really love to have carried out, such as a spacious laundry area that will accommodate a washing machine, tumble dryer, ironing board and clothes-horse to air large items, but do not try to solve problems – that is the architect's job.

Be open to new ideas and suggestions, but do not expect answers to come at once; sometimes the best solutions will emerge only after the third or fourth design draft. Make sure you are completely happy with the final brief, and that you have talked through the entire plan in detail, before giving the project the go-ahead.

Experience

Ask each architect what experience he has of designing and working with your style of property. Were the buildings of a similar size and proportion to yours? Can you see the work, and does he have before and after photos? Can you speak to the clients? Will the architect be doing the design work himself, or will he be farming it out to his staff? If so, can you meet with them?

Time and cost

How long will the design work take, and how soon can the architect start working on it? What will be the key milestones in the project? When will you start incurring costs? There can be a very large disparity between different architects' costs and designs, and many homeowners end up spending two or three times their original budget. Only you can decide whether the final results will be worth the outlay.

On large projects over £20,000, architects' fees normally amount to 10–14 per cent of the total building cost of the project. A striking extension to a large period home can cost anything from £50,000 to £150,000. Ask your architect what services are included as part of his fees, whether there will be any other design contractors' fees payable, when they will have to be paid, and the best way to draw up a budget for the construction work. Make sure the quotes include VAT costs where applicable.

Finding builders

The only way to find a good builder is by recommendation. If you do not know anyone who can recommend a builder personally, look out for building work being carried out in your neighbourhood, and knock on the owners' doors or drop a note through their letterbox. Is the work being carried out to a high standard? Do the builders arrive on time? Is their work clean and safe? Would the owners be happy to recommend them to you?

Otherwise, local councils, who grant planning permission, may be able to recommend someone. Ask your architect if he can recommend builders. If a major project is being carried out, such as a garage being built on to the side of your house, and an extra bedroom on top, you may need to hire a project manager to oversee the smooth running and completion of the work. Some architects will oversee a project themselves.

Kitchens

Well-appointed, cosy, open-plan kitchens often form the heart and soul of modern family homes. These days, even trendy young professionals who may only use kitchens for storing wine and boiling the occasional egg demand classy-looking kitchen appliances and units. So when choosing a new kitchen, pick the best materials and units you can afford, but do not spend more than 10 per cent of the value of your property. Provided your spend is in proportion to the value of your property, you should recoup about 70 per cent of your investment when you come to sell your home.

Installing a new kitchen is expensive and disruptive, so select a layout and design that will not date too quickly, and will appeal to as wide a market as possible. Classic wood combined with stainless steel units or frosted glass looks both modern and traditional, and will appeal to most buyers. When planning a timescale for the installation to be carried out, remember that deliveries of fittings can take up to eight weeks, so place your order as soon as you have made your selection.

The layout

There are many software packages available that will allow you to scan in a photograph of your kitchen, bathroom or any other room you are redecorating and experiment with different layouts and colour schemes. When designing your kitchen remember that the sink, dishwasher and washing machine should be installed as close to the soil pipe on the outside of the building as possible. You should also note where the existing electricity points and gas supply outlets are located, as moving these will be expensive too. Ideally you should have an electrical socket for every kitchen appliance, large and small. Organise your kitchen ergonomically. Most women like the workspace to be arranged triangularly so food can be taken out of the fridge, put into the sink, and on to the hob or oven.

Joinery

Kitchen store cupboards (technically known as carcasses) suffer a lot of wear and tear and have to bear a lot of weight, so when examining specifications look out for signs of scratching and chipping. Good-quality ready-made cabinets are better than cheap flat-packed ones. Opt for drawers that are built on metal rather than plastic runners.

Modern kitchen cabinets can come with a range of interior fittings such as pull-out baskets, magic corner carousels, pan and bottle racks and plate pegs on doors that will make everyday tasks much easier, and can transform the smallest of kitchens into super-organised culinary workspaces. Cabinet doors come in a wide range of materials – from ultra-contemporary stainless steel to wood, lacquer, laminate and veneer, and should be chosen to match the flooring and work surfaces.

Flooring

Kitchen floors accumulate an awful lot of grease, dirt and spillages, so they need to be hardwearing, non-slippery and easy to clean. Avoid surfaces that require waxing or scrubbing. The overall appearance of your kitchen should be harmonious and coherent, so choose flooring that will complement the cupboards, walls and work surfaces. As I explained in the last chapter, a good way of creating harmony is to decide on a theme and carry it through the floors, cupboards, walls, furnishings and splashbacks.

Work surfaces

Kitchen worktops are used for cutting, grinding, chopping and slicing food, and need to be the most hardwearing part of the kitchen. They can also radically alter the appearance of the room. If you have opted for plain, inexpensive kitchen cupboards, installing a thick, luxurious work surface can really lift the overall appearance of your kitchen, and give your kitchen a designer look – but on a budget.

When it comes to choosing material for the worktops, granite is fashionable and heat-resistant, but expensive and heavy; ceramic tiles are decorative, but prone to trapping dirt in the grouting; hardwood looks and feels lovely, but requires regular seasoning with oil; stainless steel is hygienic, easy to clean and water- and heat-resistant, but can easily be marked and scratched and is noisy; and laminate is cheap and comes in numerous designs but, unless you choose a high-pressure one, it will not be heatproof and will allow water to penetrate through the seams.

The appliances

Decide what appliances you want in your kitchen at the planning stage, so that you can incorporate them into the overall design.

Built-in cookers, fridges and dishwashers will give your kitchen the much-desired streamlined look, but free-standing ones that can easily be replaced and repaired, and taken with you when you leave, are also making a comeback.

If you need a tall, family-sized fridge/freezer it should be wedged in a corner between two walls, as it will look bulky and odd if it is placed between a row of fitted cupboards.

Bathrooms

Though important, new bathrooms will not give as high a return on a home as a new kitchen, so spend no more than 7 per cent of the property's value on a new bathroom, and expect to recoup about 60 per cent of your investment when you move.

Bathroom fixtures are relatively cheap – you can pick up a suite for as little as £200, so the bulk of your budget will be swallowed up by the cost of plumbing and installation. As I said in the last chapter, bathroom suites must be white, but you can create creative and dazzling effects through the use of coloured splashbacks and smart finishings and accessories.

Planning and building regulations in relation to bathrooms

Bathroom fittings are permanent fixtures, so experiment with the layout of the room until you are sure you are happy with it. Start by locating the existing plumbing and radiators – the loo should be positioned as closely as possible to the outside soil pipe. Any alterations you make to the plumbing must comply with the by-laws administered by your local water authority, and any changes to the drainage and waste system must comply with building regulations.

You must also obtain building regulations approval if you want to create a brand-new bathroom anywhere in the property. One of the regulation requirements is that you must have an extractor fan wired to the light switch to provide adequate ventilation. If you are not sure if your plans meet the necessary requirements or are practicable, consult a qualified architect, surveyor or plumber. Most bathroom showrooms on the high street will offer a planning and installation service, but this will add considerably to the overall cost of the project.

Baths

No matter how small your bathroom is, fit in a bath if you can. A standard bath measures 1700mm by 700mm, but smaller and larger designs are available. If your bathroom is an awkward shape, a corner bath can work well. If you are really pushed for space, install a sit-in bath, which can be squeezed into virtually any corner. As mentioned in the last chapter, a free-standing Victorian-style bath with traditional brass mixer taps and shower attachments looks very elegant. Cast-iron baths also look classy, but are expensive.

Showers

Ideally, every bathroom will have a separate bath and shower cubicle, but if this is not possible, install one over the bath. A power shower is highly desirable, but check that you have the right type of boiler first. You will need to fit a pump to the water supply to the shower, which is not feasible with combination boilers.

If your property has a combination boiler, it is better to install a separate electric shower, which heats up cold water independently from the boiler, or you will get little more than a trickle. Shower curtains are a nuisance and quickly become mouldy, so fit a glass shower screen if you can.

Wet rooms, which are small rooms that have been turned into walk-in showers by tiling the entire floor area on a slight slope so that the water runs down the drain hole, are the ultimate status symbol in classy modern flats and loft apartments.

Basins and taps

Pedestal basins come in a range of styles and shapes. A wall-mounted basin with a well-organised storage cupboard beneath it will give the room a neat profile. Your choice of taps is as important as your choice of suite fittings and will impact on the overall appearance of your bathroom. Chrome always looks elegant, but whichever style and finish you go for, buy mixer taps for the basin and the bath, to add a touch of luxury.

En-suite bathrooms and a downstairs cloakroom

Many families these days demand an extra bathroom off the master bedroom as a matter of course, so if you have room, adding an en-suite will certainly add to the value of your property. Ideally the second bathroom will have a full bath and shower cubicle, but if you are really short of space, a shower, basin and loo will do. A downstairs loo is also much appreciated by families.

The exterior of the property

As I said in the last chapter, looking after the exterior of your property is crucial if you want to maintain its optimum value.

Windows

Windows must be in keeping with both the architectural style of your property and your neighbourhood. The wrong windows in the wrong property or area will automatically shave several thousand pounds off the value of your home.

Walk down your street or local neighbourhood and see what type of window has been installed in the most expensive properties. Do the majority of the properties have UPVC double-glazed windows, or traditional sash boxes? UPVC double-glazed windows, which look attractive and are cheap, durable and easy to maintain, tend to add value to those properties built after 1900.

New sash windows, which look lovely in period properties, will cost at least £1,800 each, but are a worthwhile investment if they are in keeping with the style of the property and area. Two types of windows that should be replaced immediately are steel windows, which are prone to condensation and rust, and louvre windows, which were popular in the 1970s but pose a serious security risk because the glass slates can easily be removed.

Porches

A small, enclosed porch area around the front door of a house can make an attractive and secure entrance to a home, and will also reduce draughts and provide extra insulation. Porches are also ideal spaces for hanging up wet coats, umbrellas, shoes, and reducing the amount of condensation brought into the home.

Porches must conform to building regulations, but provided the floor area does not exceed 2sqm, and the door does not exceed 3m, you do not need to seek planning permission. Your porch door will become your new front door so make sure it has a letterbox, doorbell and number plate. An obscured glass panel is a good security feature, particularly when you are away on holiday and mail is piling up.

Garages

Most car owners would prefer to park their car in a dry, secure garage than on an exposed driveway, or worse on the street. A garage can also double up as a utility room for noisy washing machines and tumbledryers and bulky freezers, and storage room for gardening and DIY tools.

The ideal site for a garage is to the side of the property that does not have windows, so that it will not block light from coming into the house or spoil the view. To park a car, your garage must have a minimum width of 2.4m to allow ample room for passenger doors to open. If the garage is to double up as a utility area, you will also need to allow for elbow room.

As with all other improvements, the style and design of the garage should blend in with the style of the house. Having a custom-designed garage built can cost as much as an extension, but there is a wide choice of readymade garage kits on offer, in a range of different materials.

Routine maintenance

When it comes to the day-to-day maintenance of her property, little and often should be the mantra of the property goddess. Get to know your property by creating a 'home management file'. Make a note of where the stopcock, gas, electricity and water meters are located, and learn how to operate them in an emergency. In addition, check your property regularly for signs of damp and rot, and keep condensation to a minimum by keeping bathrooms and kitchens well ventilated.

Damp

If water can seep into your property either from above through a leak in the roof or gutters (known as penetrating damp), or through the floor or walls (known as rising damp), it will rapidly deteriorate the fabric of your property, so learn to spot tell tale signs, and attend to them immediately. The three main ways in which water can *penetrate* into a home are:

Roof tiles

Roof tiles can slip or crack during a freak storm, sudden burst of thunder or lightning, so if you live in a house or top floor flat get into the habit of checking the roof from the front, back and sides of the property regularly, particularly during the winter months. Defective tiles should be repaired immediately to avoid water seeping into the ceiling and walls. If several tiles have become damaged and the roof is ageing it may require a complete overhaul.

Flashings

The joints where the roof and walls meet are usually protected by a layer of lead known as flashing. When the flashing becomes damaged by weather it can also allow water to seep into joints between the ceiling and walls, and cause wallpaper and paintwork to peel and stain.

Gutters

If gutters are broken or become blocked with leaves and debris, water will clog up and seep into the property.

Rising damp

If paintwork is starting to blister or wallpaper is starting to peel off the walls, ground water may be creeping through the floors and up the walls of the property. This is known as *rising damp*. Rising damp can occur due to a ruptured or non-existent damp proof course; leaks in plumbing or central heating; moulded soil resting against the sides of the property; blocked drains; or water creeping into the property from underneath the window sills.

Few things strike more fear into the heart of a homeowner than the prospect of their property suffering from rising damp. However, specialist damp companies are prone to scaremongering. If there are no visible signs of deterioration on the inside and the property does not feel damp, the problem is unlikely to be as serious as an over-zealous specialist (or surveyor) may lead you to believe. In fact, there may not be a problem with damp at all. In such cases, there is no need to fork out several hundreds of pounds on a new chemical damp proof course. Simply keeping the exterior brickwork, drains, gutters and window ledges in good condition and interior of your property well ventilated, will suffice.

Damp proof courses

If water clearly is creeping into the interior of your property and the walls show signs of rising damp, contact several damp specialists to provide a report on the problem and give you an estimate for building a damp proof course. A damp proof course is created by injecting silicon resin into the wall and replacing the internal plaster with waterproof plaster.

In addition to creating a damp proof course, you can mitigate the problem of ground water creeping into the property by sloping paths and surfaces away from the walls, so rainwater flows directly into the drains rather than remaining on the surface. Remove soil resting against the wall of the property. Airbricks ventilate the space above and below the floor and help prevent damp and condensation, so ensure that the holes are free of blockages.

Rot

Failing to prevent damp rising or penetrating into your property can lead to problems of rot in the timbers. There are two main types of rot: *wet rot* and *dry rot*. The latter is the most serious and expensive to treat.

Wet rot can affect any untreated timber that has been exposed to prolonged damp. Window and door frames that are not painted regularly are particularly susceptible to wet rot. The symptoms are easy to spot, as the wood starts to feel soft, wet and flaky. However, wet rot can be easily treated by a general builder or timber specialist.

Dry rot is altogether more difficult to spot in the initial stages and expensive to treat. Dry rot is a fungus that attacks and breaks down wood that has high moisture content. It is highly cancerous and can spread into bricks and masonry. Once dry rot has become established it is easy to spot as it looks like a flat, fluffy white layer of pancake that can be peeled away. Dry rot is treated by removing and replacing all the affected woodwork, and treating the surrounding timbers and masonry with a chemical preventative – an expensive and difficult job.

Condensation

Condensation occurs when the moisture content in a room is high and the surfaces and air is cold. The vapours caused by cooking, bathing and just breathing, condense back into water when they touch cold surfaces such as bathroom walls and windows. Condensation causes patches of mould to form on walls and surfaces, and can quickly encourage rot in timbers. It is also very bad for your lungs.

The average family produces 20 pints of water vapour a day, so every home has some condensation. However, if mould patches are forming on the walls and surfaces feel wet, the problem is serious and the property requires better ventilation and insulation. Double-glazing, loft and cavity wall insulation all help to keep condensation at bay.

In addition, you should install extractor fans in the kitchen and bathrooms, or close doors when cooking and showering, but open the windows. Use lids when cooking to cut down on the amount of steam escaping into the air, and dry clothes outside or in a tumbledryer vented to the outside. If you must dry clothes inside, ensure that the room is well ventilated and do not use a gas heater to speed up the drying process, as it gives off a lot of water.

Summary

Having bought her home, the property goddess ensures that every change she makes to the décor, fixtures and fittings, structure and layout of the property adds value to her home.

1) The top five improvements that add value to a property are:
   a) gas central heating
   b) kitchens and bathrooms
   c) extensions and conservatories
   d) loft conversions
   e) garages.

2) Kitchens and bathrooms.
   a) Use software packages to experiment with layout and colour schemes.
   b) Sinks, dishwashers, and lavatories must be located close to water supply/soil pipes.
   c) Choose classic designs that will appeal to as wide a market as possible.

3) Loft conversions and extensions.
   a) Find out if you will need planning permission.

b) Ensure that your designs satisfy health and safety requirements, and comply with fire safety regulations.

c) Do not over-extend your property.

4) Architects and builders:
   a) Discuss all the compromises you have had to make in your property with your architect.
   b) Do not expect solutions to come at once.
   c) Remember the only way to find a good builder is by recommendation.

5) Routine Maintenance:
   a) Little and often is the mantra of the property goddess.
   b) Check your property regularly for signs of condensation, rot and damp.

5

Investing

Buying properties and letting them out to tenants, commonly known as 'buy-to-let', has become very popular as a form of investment in recent years, as property prices have soared and share prices faltered. The idea of buy-to-let is that the tenants' rent payments will cover your mortgage and maintenance costs, and as property prices appreciate, the capital value of your property portfolio will rise too.

With multinational companies relocating out of large cities, a rising student population, an influx of workers from those European countries that have recently joined the EU, and a growing number of potential first-time buyers who are still renting accommodation well into their thirties, the prognosis for buy-to-let investors is good, but only if you select your locations and properties wisely.

In this chapter, we will see how to win at the buy-to-let game by focusing on locations likely to deliver good income yields, and avoiding those already drowning in a surplus of rental accommodation. We will see where to find the best buy-to-let mortgages; how to offset business expenses against income tax; and to shelter profits from capital gains tax. We will also explore how to find a good lettings agent; your rights and responsibilities as a landlord; and the importance of insuring, maintaining and managing your rental properties well.

The two laws of property investment

Successful property investment is not rocket science, but it does require time, commitment and research. In the same way as many investors who piled money into dotcoms had their fingers burnt when the technology bubble burst, many thousands of amateur landlords who have jumped on the buy-to-let bandwagon – in the hope of earning some easy money – are finding themselves lumbered with large mortgages on properties that they cannot let or sell.

If you are seriously considering becoming a property investor, ask yourself if you can fulfil the two laws of the game:

1 Are you prepared to dedicate time, money and research to developing a business?
2 Can you afford to tie up your money for the long term?

1 Property investment is a business requiring time, money and research

Buying and selling property for investment is different to buying and selling property for your own use, because first and foremost property investment is a *business* and, like any other business, it requires a sound business plan. All the property skills I have outlined so far – drawing up a checklist of exactly what you want in terms of accommodation; researching the location; planning your finances; carrying out improvements that will add value to your properties; and being able to sell your properties quickly and profitably – are crucial to the property investor.

In addition, you will also need to pay far more attention to market timing and respond to changing economic conditions, because – as with any other type of investing – your aim is to buy when house prices are *falling* and sell when they are *rising*. As a property investor you are running a *service business* – providing homes to clients who need accommodation; and for any service business to succeed, it must be operating in a market in which *demand* is *high*, but *supply* is *low*.

In many parts of London, letting agents report that their books are overflowing with private rental properties for which they cannot find tenants. This has led to a spate of press reports suggesting that the 'buy-to-let bubble is about to burst'. The reality is that there *is* money to be made from buying to let, but not in areas where the rental market is saturated – unless you are only seeking long-term capital gains.

First you will need to decide on your *niche market*. People who rent accommodation can generally be split into six groups: social housing tenants; students; young graduate sharers; single professionals; families; and corporate tenants. Generally speaking, properties at the lower end of the market tend to yield better income returns than those at the higher end. But whatever market you choose, your success in finding tenants will depend largely on how well your properties meet their requirements in terms of location, accommodation, décor, fixtures and furnishings, so researching your market's needs is crucial.

You will need to make financial projections as to your *income and capital yields*, keep careful business accounts, and insure your properties adequately. To ensure that your rental properties remain marketable, satisfy health and safety regulations, and can be sold quickly and profitably when you want to release your capital, it is also vital that you keep them in good repair, attend to any maintenance work promptly, and redecorate periodically. If you haven't a clue where the stopcock is located in your own home, or wouldn't be able to find a plumber at short notice, you're probably not quite ready to become a property investor!

2 Running a property business is a long-term investment

As we have seen in previous chapters, buying and selling property is expensive and time-consuming. Unlike stocks and shares that can be sold in a matter of minutes by phoning a broker, property cannot be sold at the drop of a hat. To release capital tied up in an investment property, you would have to give notice to any tenants living there, put the property on the market, find a buyer, and wait several weeks for all the legal work to be completed, before getting your hands on your cash.

Like all commodities, the property market goes through economic cycles, and if you find yourself trapped in a position where you need to sell a property when prices are falling, you could end up making a significant financial loss. This is every property investor's worst nightmare, and the sorry position that many amateur landlords could find themselves in. Investing in bricks and mortar is a long-term game and not something that you should consider unless you can afford to tie up your money for at least ten, or preferably fifteen, years.

Ten steps to becoming a successful property investor

If you are looking to invest for the long term, and are prepared to put in the necessary time and legwork in researching locations, finding the right properties, then managing and maintaining them, there is no reason why you should not start building up a property portfolio. To help you get started, follow our ten-point plan.

1 Location, location, location

To make a success out of property investment you must buy in areas in which demand for rental accommodation outstrips supply, and where you are likely to achieve *high income yields*. Start by drawing up a long list of locations you feel might deliver good returns for whatever reason – a large student population, being close to hospitals, opening of a new research centre, new transport links, etc. Then examine trends in property prices and rental incomes in the area over several years. Have the rental payments been high in comparison to property prices?

Study reports on the state of the rental market in the area, and take advice from local lettings agents who are members of the Association of Residential Lettings Agents (ARLA), the professional body for the private rental sector. Become an expert on the areas you are planning to invest in. Which parts of town are most popular with students, nurses and young doctors? Are there any changes in the pipeline that may have an adverse effect on rental incomes in the near future, such as the proposed relocation of a university faculty or the closure of a hospital wing?

Avoid London and other expensive areas
Research by Paragon Mortgages shows that the average rent paid by tenants across the UK in 2003 was £450 a month, and that only 12 per cent of tenants paid more than £800 a month. So investing in areas such as London, the south-east, Birmingham, Bristol, Manchester and Leeds, where two-bedroom flats frequently let for more than £450 *a week*, does not make good business sense.

Not only is there a worrying oversupply of private rental accommodation in many parts of London (in some areas, estate agents report that they have more properties on their books available to let than for sale), rental properties in London also tend to remain empty for longer than in other areas. So unless you can afford to maintain monthly payments on two or three large mortgages in addition to your own, with no additional income coming in for several weeks of the year, avoid London and other expensive towns and cities.

Look for cheap properties that generate high-income yields

Over the last couple of years, investors have been turning their attentions to the north-east region of England – in particular, the areas two miles either side of the Tyne, where there is a strong tradition of renting accommodation and tenants are plentiful. At the social housing end of the spectrum, investors can buy flats for well under £100,000 and achieve rental yields of up to 15 per cent a year, which compares well with property prices of over £250,000 and income yields of less than 3 per cent in central London.

Other areas worth considering are the cities of Portsmouth, Southampton and Bournemouth, where there is strong demand for rental properties from students. In many cases, universities will take on properties on a five-year basis; guarantee the rent; and promise to return the property in good condition at the end of the contractual period.

During 2003, there was a huge increase in demand for rental properties from doctors and nurses moving into the Shrewsbury area. Reports also showed that there was a shortage of rental accommodation in the city of Winchester, where tenants were queuing up to sign leases on good rental properties.

The town of Ashford in Kent has become popular with investors, due to an increase in building activity and plans for a new London rail link for the Channel Tunnel. But be wary of jumping the gun and investing in neglected areas on the whim of proposed long-term transport plans. In 2001, there was much excitement about plans to extend the East London tube line down to West Croydon. However, by 2004, serious doubts began to surface as to whether the extension would actually go ahead and regenerate vast swathes of south-east London.

Make friends with a local ARLA agent

The idea of 'buying to let' really caught on as an investment vehicle in the mid-1990s, following initiatives by ARLA to stimulate growth in the private rental market. In 1996, ARLA launched a campaign to encourage more small investors into the private rental market by publishing a raft of simple guides on how to make property investment work for the average person on the street. It also persuaded mortgage lenders to offer cheaper mortgages to investors, and there is now an array of competitively priced buy-to-let mortgages on the market.

ARLA has more than 1,200 member offices in the UK. Many employ sales' agents or work closely with local estate agents, who can search for properties with lettings' potential on an investor's behalf. They can also advise on the level of rents you could hope to achieve, whether you should make changes to the décor and accommodation to suit the prevailing needs of the market, and what sort of fixtures and furnishings you should provide. This is invaluable advice, so having narrowed down your long list of locations, contact local ARLA agents for help with finding suitable properties and preparing them for the rental market. If they can see that you are a serious investor who is likely to buy and let through them, you're likely to find them extremely helpful.

2 Decide on your niche market

Tenants tend to fall into one of six social categories. Each group has its advantages and disadvantages.

Social housing tenants

Letting in this sector will generate the highest income yields, though this sector is often the most 'challenging' in terms of dealing with tenants, collecting rent, and keeping properties in good repair. Although purchase prices in London are still higher than in other parts of the country, this is one sector where demand for properties is still very strong in many areas of London, and investors can achieve good income yields. Former local authority properties yield between 8 per cent and 9 per cent a year, while flats in high-rise blocks are generating yields of more than 10 per cent a year.

Easylease is a government-funded, council-run scheme that can help prospective investors find suitable properties to let. It was set up by a group of London boroughs to encourage more private landlords to make properties available to the homeless, many of whom were previously being housed in expensive bed and breakfast accommodation.

Unlike private lettings agents, it does not charge landlords commission to place tenants, and the rent is paid by the council, so you are unlikely to suffer long delays in receiving money. Easylease also takes care of all internal repairs, and guarantees to return the property in its original condition at the end of the agreed term. Such is the demand for more properties in this sector that, as an added incentive, many local authorities will even pay landlords a signature fee of up to £6,000 upon signing a lease.

Students, young graduate sharers, single professionals and families

While professional singles and couples usually rent one-bedroom *flats*, most students, young graduate professionals and families require *houses*.

The advantage of investing in houses rather than flats is the flexibility. A good three-bedroom house in a large town or city with a university, several hospitals and multinational companies can be let to a group of three to six students, and refurbished and redecorated to let to three young working professionals, or a young family.

Not only do houses also tend to appreciate more than flats, they are also much easier to sell on to private buyers than one-bedroom flats. Research by the Alliance & Leicester shows that more than 60 per cent of first-time buyers preferred two-bedroom properties to one-bedroom properties. Many investors who purchase one-bedroom flats find that they can only sell them on to other investors when they want to release their capital, which narrows their market significantly. While property developers are building rafts of smart new apartment blocks in towns and cities across the country, there are fewer new family houses being built, so demand for good three- and four-bedroom Victorian houses is likely to remain very consistent.

People who rent accommodation tend to rent the minimum they require, whereas those who buy think long term and buy the maximum they can afford. Therefore one-bedroom flats are always easier to let to singles or couples than two-bedroom flats, although – as we have seen – they are much harder to sell. Smart one-bedroom flats are far less flexible investments than houses, so be sure that demand for such accommodation is consistent over the long term before buying.

Corporate tenants

At the top end of the rental market are corporate tenants, whose employers pay top prices for swanky accommodation. While corporate leases are often longer than standard contracts, and the rent is more secure because it is coming from the employer rather than the tenant, such properties are expensive to purchase and rental demand is very much dependent on the vicissitudes of the economic market. American executives traditionally account for 34 per cent of the corporate market in London; however, following the war in Iraq, this slumped to just 18 per cent. So this sector is more suited to wealthy investors looking for long-term capital growth (as opposed to high annual income yields) rather than first-time investors.

Corporate tenants comprise families relocating to a new city, and young, single executives. Families look for houses close to international schools, amenities and public transport, and tend to demand large fridges and freezers, separate washing machines and tumble dryers, well-equipped family kitchens, safe, tidy gardens, and quality décor finished to a good professional standard. Single executives look for smart modern flats with wet rooms, gleaming kitchen appliances, off-street parking and good security.

Don't put all your eggs in one basket!

Whichever sector of the rental market you opt for, be sure to spread the risk and not put all your money in one basket. If you have £150,000 to invest, buy three small flats for £50,000 each, rather than one house for £150,000. If you have researched your market well, it is unlikely that all three properties will be empty at the same time, which will mitigate cash-flow problems. Spreading your investment across several properties also gives you the flexibility to sell one property and re-invest in another, if you discover that one particular property is not yielding the returns you hoped for, or you just want to expand your portfolio.

3 Work out the income yields

As I have said, every property investor needs to ensure that the tenants' rental payments will cover their mortgage and insurance expenses, plus the cost of managing and maintaining the properties. The profit you make on your properties after paying the mortgage, insurance, management and maintenance fees is known as the *net yield*.

Gross yield

To work out the net yield on an investment property, you first need to work out the *gross yield* by dividing the market value of your property by the annual rental payments, and multiplying the figure by 100, to give you a percentage. So, if you buy a flat for £150,000 and let it for £900 a month, your annual rental income will be £10,800. Divide this by £150,000 and multiply the figure by 100, and you get 7.2 per cent. This is the *gross yield*.

When developers quote in their marketing literature an attractive 'guaranteed income yield' for new properties under construction, their figures usually correspond to the projected *gross yield* an investor could achieve. However, this figure is misleading, as it does not take into account the cost of insuring, maintaining and furnishing the property, and paying the mortgage during the inevitable void periods.

Net income yield

So to obtain a more realistic evaluation, you need to work out the *net income yield* – that is, your annual income minus your business expenses. To do this, take your annual rent, and deduct all the expenses you will incur in keeping and letting the property, excluding your mortgage payments. If you are a fairly bullish investor, factor in at least two weeks' void period; if you are more cautious, factor in four weeks. So, the annual costs on our £150,000 flat might go as follows:

Service charges: £700
Ground Rent: £150
Buildings insurance: £250
Maintenance and repair: £3,500
Letting agents' fees (15 per cent of rental income): £1,620
Two weeks' void period: £400
Total: £6,620

To work out the net yield, deduct the total sum of all your business expenses from your annual rental income of £10,800 (£4,180), divide it by the capital value of the property, and multiply it by 100, and you are left with a net income yield of 2.78 per cent. The higher the income yield, the less likely you are to experience cash-flow problems.

Do not buy properties that will yield a net income of less than 4 per cent. Experts generally only recommend investing in rental properties that will achieve a *net income yield of at least 4 per cent,* unless you have very deep cash reserves you can dip into. So, going on these figures, this particular flat would probably not make a great rental investment.

Property investor Ajay Ahuja, who bought his first flat at the age of twenty-four, abides by a very simple formula to assess a property's investment potential. He says: 'Take the purchase price and knock off the last two zeros – that is the figure you should be able to achieve in rent each month. So, if you see a flat for £90,000 and know you can get £900 a month or more in rent, buy it. If you would only get £700, walk away.' Ahuja now owns over sixty properties and his empire is worth several million pounds, so the theory seems to have worked for him!

4 Work out the capital yields

But income yields are only one part of the story. Most investors are attracted to property because history shows that prices appreciate over the long term. The average property purchased for £25,000 in 1980 could have been sold ten years later for well over £68,000 – a return of over 270 per cent. Property prices have soared over the past couple of years. However, as we saw in the late 1980s, they can also crash.

The financial gain you make between buying and selling properties in your portfolio is your capital profit. But again, you have to factor in all the business expenses associated with buying and selling property, such as stamp duty, searches, estate agents' and legal fees.

On top of these, you also have to factor in the cost of taxation. The Inland Revue levies capital gains tax at 40 per cent on profits made on the sale of any property that is not your main residence. So if you sold your £150,000 property for £350,000 ten years later, you might have a tax bill of £80,000. As of April 2005, it will be possible to shelter property from tax by putting it in a personal pension, and I explain this in more detail later in the chapter.

No investor can project capital yields in the same way as they can with income yields, as they cannot be sure by how much property prices will rise or fall in the future. This is why it is crucial to invest in properties that will generate predictable income yields and offer flexibility over the long term.

5 Mortgages and insurance

Mortgages

To obtain a buy-to-let mortgage you will need a deposit of at least 15 per cent of the purchase price of the property, plus all the associated costs of stamp duty and legal fees. So to buy a one-bedroom flat for £65,000, you would need at least £8,500 in cash.

Because buy-to-let is seen as a business loan, unlike when lending on your principal residence, lenders will base their decision on the letting income the property is likely to generate, rather than the borrower's income. Most lenders will not agree a loan unless you can demonstrate that the property can be let for at least 130 per cent of your mortgage payments. So, if your payments on your buy-to-let mortgage come to £700 a month, you will need to convince your lender that you can let the property for at least £910 a month.

As I have already said, the buy-to-let mortgage market has expanded considerably over the past eight years, and some of the big name lenders now active in this field include: Birmingham Midshires, Bristol & West, Mortgage Express, Woolwich and the Bank of Ireland, as well as specialist lenders such as Paragon Mortgages and UCB Home Loans.

At the time of writing, some of the best deals on the market were with the Cheltenham & Gloucester, which was sporting a two-year fixed rate of 5.24 per cent with a 25 per cent deposit, and Northern Rock, which was offering a five-year fixed rate at 6.19 per cent with a 15 per cent deposit, plus a £695 set-up fee. Abbey National and the Marketplace were also offering attractive discounted and tracker rate loans.

Insurance

It is vital that you insure your investment properties adequately to protect yourself, your tenants and also third parties. Buildings and contents insurance designed for residential property is insufficient for landlords, so you should buy specialist policies that will provide cover in the following four areas:

1 *Buildings*: This should cover the full rebuild cost of the property in the case of fire, flood, lightning, smoke, aircraft

damage, etc. Many policies also cover malicious damage caused by tenants, which is invaluable if you are letting at the lower end of the social spectrum.

2 *Contents*: This should cover damage to carpets, curtains, blinds, light fixtures and fittings not covered under buildings insurance, white goods and furniture.

3 *Legal expenses*: This will cover solicitors' and court hearing expenses in the event that you need to resort to these means to remove a tenant from your property.

4 *Rent guarantee*: This will guarantee that you receive the rent agreed in the tenancy agreement, and is crucial if you have a mortgage on the property. Some policies will also cover void periods.

Have a contingency fund

No matter how well you research your location, and adapt your properties to suit the needs of the market, occasional void periods when the property is empty (but of course you still have to pay the mortgage and keep the property in good condition) are an inevitable fact of life for every landlord. It is vital that you have sufficient cash reserves to tide you over during these drought periods, so before buying your first investment property build up a contingency fund *equivalent to at least six months' mortgage payments,* to see you through the rainy days.

6 Finding tenants

I would strongly advise you to employ an ARLA registered lettings agent to manage your properties. ARLA members are required to have been in business for at least two years and to hold professional indemnity insurance cover. Members are also covered by a fidelity bond that provides financial protection to clients (landlords and tenants) in the event of their monies being misappropriated by the agent. ARLA runs regular training courses and seminars on all aspects of the lettings' industry, and keeps its members up to date on current legislation.

Do not ask friends or family to manage your property

If you do decide to go it alone, under no circumstances ask a friend or family member to look after a rental property on your behalf. Managing rental properties and looking after tenants is a full-time job that requires a range of skills, and farming out the responsibility to an inexperienced friend or family member is just asking for trouble.

If you are serious about property investing, I would even discourage you from *letting* to friends, as it is tempting to turn a blind eye to late rental payments, or minor damage to furniture, rather than rock the friendship boat, which can lead to resentment later on.

Lettings agents

Most ARLA agents offer three levels of service:

1 Finding tenants.
2 Finding tenants and collecting the rent.
3 Finding tenants, collecting the rent, and undertaking full management of the property.

Fees vary, but most agents charge between 10 per cent and 15 per cent of the rental income for a full management service. These expenses are tax deductible, and unless you have the time, experience and desire to attend to burst water pipes in the middle of the night, leaking washing machines, broken TV aerials and tenants who cannot change light bulbs, I would strongly advise you to opt for a full management service.

What a lettings agent will do

In return for their fee, lettings agents will undertake the following duties:

- *Tenant introduction and vetting*: The agent will find suitable tenants for your property, and make checks with credit reference agencies to ensure that they can meet the rental payments. They may also take up references from employers and previous landlords.
- *Inventories*: The agent will organise a full inventory of the property before a new tenant moves in and immediately after they have vacated the property. This will list all the furniture and fittings in the property, and record minor damages present at the beginning of the tenancy agreement and at the end, so the landlord can ask the tenant to make good any damage that has occurred during the tenancy, or part of the deposit withheld in lieu. The landlord usually pays for the inventory at the start of the agreement, and the tenant for the inventory at the end.
- *Rent collection*: The agent will collect rent from the tenant and ensure that it is passed on to you promptly.
- *Tenancy agreements*: The agent will draw up a tenancy agreement outlining the terms of the lease. Tenancy agreements drawn up by ARLA agents tend to be far more detailed than off-the-shelf agreements available for sale via the internet or in stationery shops. All tenancy agreements are now *assured shorthold tenancies*, so possession of the property automatically reverts to the landlord at the end of the agreement, and you can obtain a court order instructing tenants to vacate the premises if they fail to leave once the term expires.
- *Change of tenants*: The agents will also inform the local council and utility companies of a change of tenants.
- *Maintenance*: If you have opted for a full management

service, the agent will make annual inspections to ensure the property is being kept in a good condition. They will also see to any repair and maintenance problems and organise for them to be put right.

7 Your rights and responsibilities as a landlord

As a landlord, you have a duty under common law to ensure that your properties are safe and well maintained, and cannot cause injury or damage to occupants, neighbours or the general public. The structure of the property, including drains, gutters and pipes, must be in good working order, and the accommodation must be considered fit for human habitation, provide adequate heating, lighting and ventilation, and be free of damp. In addition, you should also ensure you comply with the following health and safety rules.

Gas safety
All landlords are obliged to ensure that all mains or bottled gas supplies are serviced annually by a Corgi-registered engineer, and have a certificate of safety. This certificate must be issued to the tenant on an annual basis. Failure to comply with this rule could result in a heavy fine, or even imprisonment.

Furniture fire safety
All upholstered furniture and furnishings in the property must pass the 'cigarette test', i.e. they will not burst into flames from a lit cigarette. Most furniture purchased from reputable stores after March 1990 should comply with fire safety regulations and be labelled accordingly.

Electrical safety
All electrical appliances must be safe, and you are strongly advised to have them inspected on an annual basis.

Smoke alarms

All homes built after June 1992 must have smoke detectors fitted on every floor. Although older properties are exempt, it is a good idea to have smoke alarms fitted in your properties.

Problem tenants

The two types of tenants that landlords worry about most are those who fail to pay the rent or fall into serious rent arrears, and those who cause serious, wilful damage to the property, and refuse to vacate it after you have given them notice.

Harassment and unlawful eviction

The law does protect landlords against bad tenants, and in the case of rent arrears of more than two months, or damage to the property, you can obtain a court order to have the tenants evicted. But under no circumstances attempt to evict a tenant before obtaining this document. Forcing a tenant to leave by trying to throw them out, changing the locks, tampering with their possessions or mail, or issuing verbal or physical threats, is regarded as harassment, and you could face harsh penalties and even imprisonment. Tenants have a right to peaceful enjoyment of the property they are renting, and you are required to give 24 hours' notice should you wish to enter it.

You should take basic precautions such as withholding the deposit, and including a condition in the tenancy agreement that gives you the right to end the lease on 'bad tenant' grounds. An experienced lettings agent will know when legal action is unavoidable, and can collect evidence and appear as a witness, if necessary.

8 Maintenance and repair

There should be a clause in the tenancy agreement that requires the tenant to inform the lettings agent immediately of any 'damage, disrepair, defect or deficiency' in the property, and it is vital that these are put right as soon as possible. Your property is a long-term investment, and failing to attend to problems as they occur could result in you facing huge repair bills in future years. If you have opted for a full management service, your lettings agent will organise for tradesmen to attend to the problem, settle the bill, and invoice you if necessary.

Rental properties suffer more wear and tear than privately owned homes so furnish them with sturdy curtain rails, door handles and bathroom fittings, and carpets, tiles and kitchen joinery and appliances that are hard-wearing and easy to clean. Washing machines, cookers, refrigerators, freezers and dishwashers are prone to breaking down, and will also need replacing every few years. Unless you are letting to corporate tenants, do not include linen, televisions or other entertainment systems.

9 Tax

Under present laws, rental income earned from investment properties is taxed, although certain business expenses are tax deductible. Capital gains tax of up to 40 per cent is also payable on profits made when you come to sell any property that is not your main residence. However, in early 2004, the government announced radical plans that will allow property to be held in a certain type of personal pension that is exempt from tax, as of April 2005 (see below).

Deductible business expenses

Broadly speaking, business expenses that can claimed against tax on rental income include: arrangement fees and interest on buy-to-let mortgages, insurance premiums, reasonable management costs, and the cost of wear and tear. The cost of home improvements, and the initial costs of furniture and fittings, cannot be claimed. All landlords should take professional advice from an accountant regarding their tax liabilities.

Using property as a tax-free pension

As of April 2005, you will be able to shelter your investment properties (and even your main residence and properties abroad) from income tax, capital gains tax and inheritance tax, by putting them into a self-invested personal pension (Sipp). Your properties will be held in the pension fund, along with any other investments such as investment funds you have squirrelled away into the plan for your retirement, and all profits from letting income will grow tax-free.

When you retire (any time after the age of fifty), you will have to sell any properties in the fund and use the proceeds to buy an annuity that will give you a guaranteed income for the rest of your life. For this reason, it is not advisable to put your main residence into a Sipp to protect it from inheritance tax. The costs of setting up and managing a Sipp can be high. The Inland Revenue also imposes a lifetime limit on the amount you can invest in a pension. This figure is currently £1.4 million, and any amount above this can be taxed at 60 per cent.

10 Selling your investment property

The basic rule when investing in anything, be it stocks and shares, property, or wine, *is do not enter the market until you have defined your exit route.* As I said earlier, ideally you want to buy property that you will be able to sell on to an owner-occupier rather than another investor, as this will give you a much wider market, and generally houses are much easier to sell than one-bedroom flats.

Study the buying market in the area. Is it different to the market you have been letting to? If so, what changes will you need to make to the property before putting it on the market? If the sitting room in your three-bedroom family house has been converted into a makeshift bedroom to accommodate a couple of extra students, you will have to get rid of the beds, posters and music systems and desks, and replace them with sofas, cushions and coffee tables!

Summary

Investing in property is a business, and you should not enter the market as an investor unless you can afford to tie up your money for at least ten, or preferably fifteen years.

1) Research your location carefully, by studying buy-to-let reports and talking to ARLA agents.

2) Decide on your niche market, and ensure that your properties meet their requirements.

3) Work out your income yields.

4) Find the best mortgage, buy adequate insurance, and build up a contingency fund equivalent to one year's mortgage payments.

5) Use an ARLA agent to find good tenants.

6) Ensure that your properties satisfy health and safety requirements.

7) Keep your properties in good repair.

8) Do not buy a property you would not be able to sell.

6

Buying Abroad

Over two million British people now own property abroad, and this figure is expected to soar to three million, or one in three, by 2008. Spain and France are the most popular countries, though the relaxation of foreign bureaucracy and growth in overseas mortgages mean that it is now possible to buy property almost anywhere in the world, from Dubai to the Dordogne.

In addition to purchasers of holiday-homes, the expansion of low-cost airline networks, growth of the internet, lower costs of living and a more relaxed lifestyle in many countries means the overseas' property market is attracting an increasing number of 'lifestyle buyers' who are looking to spend half the year abroad and the other half in the UK.

Another emerging trend is first-time buyers who have become priced out of the UK market and are jetting off to more affordable cities like Barcelona and Prague to sample life there and get on the property ladder. More than one in eight buyers of homes overseas are now aged between twenty-five and thirty-four.

If you have a real passion for another country, buying a

home there gives you a fantastic opportunity to immerse yourself in the local culture and lifestyle, with the added benefits of being able to cook your own meals, relax in your own sitting room, and swim in your own pool. Depending on your choice of location, you may be able to enjoy year-round sunshine, unspoilt scenery, delicious food and wine, a more appealing way of life, a lower cost of living, watersports, skiing, museums and art galleries on your doorstep. Relocating to a new country on a more permanent basis may give you the opportunity to spend more quality time with your family, raise your children in a carefree environment, become bilingual, and benefit from a better education.

But, as the never-ending streams of fly-on-the-wall documentaries frequently highlight, buying property in a foreign country without serious planning and preparation can be calamitous. Failing to research the area thoroughly, not obtaining sound, up-to-date legal advice, nor making proper checks as to the structure of the building and title of the property and land can quickly turn the dream of owning a home abroad into a living nightmare.

In this chapter I provide a basic guide to buying property in the five most popular destinations for British second-home owners: France, Italy, Spain, Portugal and the USA (mainly Florida). But before looking at each country in depth, we need to look at the five general rules that apply when buying property in any foreign country.

1 Only buy in a country towards which you feel a genuine emotional pull

Buying a home abroad should be a life-changing experience, but it is not the same as booking a holiday. Deciding to purchase a medieval town house in Dubrovnik on impulse while enjoying a bottle of local wine on a warm summer's evening could end in tears if the roof collapses in the middle of December, the builders disappear for weeks on end, and you can't communicate in Croatian.

Likewise, turning up at an overseas property fair on a rainy Sunday afternoon, and being seduced into buying an apartment off-plan in a glitzy new resort complex on the Costa Blanca, could be a disaster if the developer goes bust a few weeks later, or you find that the property bears no resemblance to the image shown in the slick marketing literature once it is finished or, even worse, that it has been built illegally.

Your home abroad will require constant finance, maintenance and repair and redecoration, just like your property at home. But this time round, you will have to fit in with local customs and ways of doing things. If you are buying in Spain, do not expect to be able to get anything done between the hours from noon to 3.30 p.m. when the entire country takes a siesta. If you have set your heart on renovating a stone wreck in Italy, do not expect builders to be forthcoming with detailed plans and estimates. In many countries, even simple things like having a new phone line installed and basic utilities connected can become a long-drawn-out affair.

The world may be your oyster in terms of opportunities, but the first rule is: *only buy in a country towards which you and your family feel a genuine emotional pull.* If you are looking for a holiday-home, do you love the locality enough to want to return to it again and again, year after year?

If want to relocate on a more permanent basis, do you have real empathy with the local people and their culture? Will you be able to cope with the language and bureaucracy? Every country has its own foibles. If you would be just as content enjoying a week's holiday in St Malo, Les Marches or Miami and venturing off somewhere else next year, you might be better off renting someone else's Breton cottage, Italian palazzo or Floridian villa.

Finding your dream home in the sun

As when searching for your dream property at home, draw up a checklist of what you are looking for in terms of location and accommodation, and log on to the internet. Having familiarised yourself with what is available in your price range, contact agents, and plan a two-week 'inspection' trip to view properties and get to know the local area. Set up your appointments from the UK to save time and ensure that you keep to a schedule.

Remember to take with you: a calculator with euro/dollar function; a mobile phone that works abroad (plus a charger); local maps; measurements of any pieces of furniture you intend to transport; a camera and a notepad; and a personal organiser to record names of estate agents, builders, and to keep track of appointments.

Once out there, get to know local people and estate agents who have been in business in the area for several years, and ask them to recommend good builders, architects and plumbers. Never make a decision to buy on the spot, and haggle hard over the purchase price – far more than you would dare to back home! Once you have decided on a property, get all your paperwork organised. Make a list of all the documentation you will need to open a bank account, obtain a mortgage and complete the purchase, and get them translated into the local language.

2 Work out how much you can afford, and plan your currency exchange

As I said in Chapter 1, the property goddess always works out how much she can afford to spend before embarking on a house-hunting mission. But budgeting to buy a property abroad is far more troublesome than budgeting to buy a property in the UK, because of the currency exchange factor.

The price of the property you wish to buy is likely to be quoted in euros or dollars, but this figure is meaningless until you have *fixed the exchange rate at which you will pay for it.* Currency markets are volatile and can change from day to day. However, even a small fluctuation in the exchange rate can add (or deduct!) several thousands of pounds to your mortgage payments and throw your initial budget way off course.

For example, during the first six months of 2003, the euro rose 15 per cent against the pound, and a €750,000 Spanish villa that would have cost £490,000 in January 2003 would have cost £528,000 in July 2003. On the other hand, the US dollar is currently languishing at a five-year low against the pound, so property in the USA is about 10 per cent cheaper than it was a few years ago.

There are three ways you can pay for your property abroad:

1 *Release equity from your home in the UK, and pay for your home abroad in cash.* If your UK property is worth £250,000 and you have a mortgage of £85,000, you could increase your mortgage to £140,000, giving you £55,000 to spend on a home in the sun, but be sure you will be able to meet the higher repayments or otherwise you will be putting your main home at risk.

2 *Take out a foreign-currency mortgage.* The Abbey National, Barclays/Woolwich, Halifax and the Norwich & Peterborough Building Society have established overseas' arms, and offer special loans to buy property in most of Europe. Rates start at 3.15 per cent in France, 3.25 per cent in Spain and 3.5 per cent in Italy and Portugal. If you are venturing further afield, mortgage broker Conti Financial Services can arrange finance to buy property in most countries. You will need a deposit of at least 25 per cent, and lenders will generally advance

3.5 times your salary minus the value of your existing mortgage.

3 *Take out a sterling-denominated mortgage on your home abroad.* Some British lenders, such as the Norwich & Peterborough Building Society, offer sterling-denominated mortgages to buy property in places like the Costa del Sol. Although the rates are a few per cent higher than those on euro mortgages, borrowing in sterling does erase the currency risk.

If you decide on either of the first two options, you will be paying for your property in a foreign currency and hence exposing yourself to currency exchange risk, so start monitoring exchange rates for the currency you require, and when you think the time is right, bite the bullet and buy all the currency you will need to complete the sale (full purchase price of the property, plus legal fees and taxes, which can add an extra 20 per cent of the purchase price to the final bill).

If you are taking on a mortgage and do not have sufficient funds to complete the sale at the outset, most banks will allow you to 'reserve' the money you need at the prevailing exchange rate for use at a future date, in return for a small deposit. Once you have bought your currency, stop monitoring the rate to see if you could have saved yourself money by waiting – it will irritate you no end and only add to the stress of the whole buying experience. Unless you are highly experienced in playing the currency markets and have a healthy capacity for risk-taking, it is unwise to speculate on currency exchange when buying property abroad.

Regardless of whether you obtain a sterling or foreign-currency mortgage, you should open a bank account in the country in which you are buying in order to pay bills, withdraw cash and pay in rental income, and always ensure you have sufficient cash reserves in both sterling and the foreign currency. If possible, choose a bank that has a branch somewhere in the UK and offers an online banking facility.

3 Obtain reliable legal advice

Getting to grips with the legalities of buying a home in England can be complicated enough. But buying a property in France, Italy, Spain, or even the USA can be twice as baffling, so it is absolutely vital to obtain reliable, up-to-date legal advice before signing on the dotted line.

Before even starting to look at properties, familiarise yourself with the buying procedures, real-estate laws and bureaucratic regimes of the country you are interested in. In Spain and France, you are liable for any debts you inherit with a property, so if your vendor fails to discharge his existing mortgage on his home before selling, you will be responsible for payments on his loan as well as your own! In some countries your home can be repossessed if you fail to pay your utility bills for a short time.

Most UK lenders offering overseas' mortgages have local, English-speaking lawyers you can employ to guide you through all the potential pitfalls of buying in your chosen country, and protect your interests. Otherwise, personal recommendation is the best way of finding a competent legal representative abroad. One of the biggest mistakes you can make is to only seek legal advice when things start to go wrong!

4 Decide how you are going to use the property

If you are just looking for a holiday bolthole, a purpose-built apartment that you can lock up and leave at the end of the summer may be more practical than a 100-year-old Spanish *finca* standing in several acres of garden, with olive groves, lemon trees and a swimming pool to maintain.

If you are planning to let your property, remember that you will achieve the highest rental income during peak season, so you might be restricted to enjoying your home in the off-peak periods, or risk losing income. Buy in an area that is within reasonable driving distance from the airport (no more than an hour), and close to a sizeable town. Access to essential amenities is an important criteria for people renting a holiday home, particularly if they have young children.

Spending half the year abroad and the remainder in the UK is an appealing lifestyle choice, but will you be able to juggle the logistics of letting a property in the UK *and* abroad, and relocating your life back and forth every six months? Will you be able to find work in both countries? If you are planning to set up a business and educate your children in your new country, what bureaucratic hurdles will you face? Will you become a foreign resident? What are the tax implications of doing this?

5 Think about the day when you will want to sell

As when buying an investment property, look ahead to the day when you will want to sell your home abroad. Is the property likely to have appreciated in value sufficiently to offset all the taxes and costs of buying and selling? In Florida it is virtually impossible to make a profit on a house sale, as there are so many new developments springing up everywhere and buyers prefer brand-new homes.

If you are buying a wreck to renovate, how easy will it be to sell the restored property ten or fifteen years later? While traditional stone farmhouses in Tuscany are in short supply, and a fully renovated property should be relatively easy to let and sell, the same is not true in all parts of France where it can be very difficult to sell an old home that has doubled or tripled in value as a result of renovations.

Think about how the surrounding area and the buyers' market (both local and overseas) may change, and therefore affect the marketability of your property in years to come. Familiarise yourself with the inheritance tax laws of the country you want to buy in (in France and Italy property is usually passed on to your children rather than your spouse, regardless of what provisions have been made in your British will), but remember that these can change in future years too.

First-time buyers

While it is virtually impossible to find a decent property in many English towns or cities for under £100,000, a budget of £70,000 would comfortably buy you a two-bedroom apartment in central Prague, a restored house in northern France, or a new-build starter home in Spain. Even in notoriously expensive cities like Paris, it is possible to pick up a one- or two-bedroom apartment in a good district for under £150,000. So if you speak a foreign language and want to work abroad or can run your business from your laptop and telephone, you might want to buy your first home abroad.

Unlike buying in the UK, you will need a deposit of at least 15 per cent of the purchase price. However, you may well find it easier to obtain a mortgage as a first-time buyer than an aspirant second-home owner who is already servicing a large mortgage on their main residence in Britain.

Prices are rising fast in many overseas' hotspots, so you may make a profit if you sell in five or six years' time, particularly if you buy in an up-and-coming country like Croatia. And, of course, once you are on the property ladder, you will find it much easier to buy another property in the UK. Unless you plan to work abroad all year round, choose a property that offers good letting potential. Cities such as Paris, Rome and Barcelona are a good long-term investment.

France

An estimated 500,000 British people currently own property in France. France is Britain's closest foreign neighbour in terms of geography at least, and is a vast and varied country in terms of climate, geography, culture and cuisine. Depending on your choice of region, you can live by the sea and mountains, deep among vineyards, forests and farmland, or in one of the country's fascinating and beautiful cities. The Loire is considered to be the dividing line between the cooler regions to the north and the warmer ones to the south. Although property prices have risen in many regions over the past five years, on balance property in France still represents good value, and has eternal appeal for those who love the culture and language, the relaxed way of life, and the superb food and wines.

The regions, properties and prices

Paris

The capital city of Paris is chic and elegant, and offers world-famous museums, art galleries, modern architecture, excellent restaurants and fashion. As in most countries, property in the capital city and surrounding areas is more expensive than elsewhere in France, but an apartment in one of the central districts of Paris is a good long-term investment as rental properties are in short supply and it is normal for French people to rent accommodation well into their thirties and forties.

There are more than 200 estate agents in Paris, and most only cover a small area, so you will have to put in a lot of legwork to find the right property in the right location. The city is split into 20 *arrondissements*, spiralling out from the historic Ile de la Cité, in the centre. The infamous River Seine runs across the middle of the city and dissects it into two distinct halves: the left bank, which is associated with intellectual debate and philosophy; and the right bank, which is now the centre of commerce and fashion.

The 1st *arrondissement* is the most central and prestigious, and property here is small and expensive. An elegant studio flat with a galleried bedroom in a seventeenth-century building will set you back at least £100,000. The fashionable Marias district to the east, which is full of unusual boutiques and fashionable bars, is slightly cheaper and popular with students. You can pick up a studio here for £65,000, or a one-bedroom apartment with a generous reception room for £120,000. The leafy district of Montmartre is just a ten-minute ride from the Gard du Nord, and is less touristy than the more central districts. This area is steeped in artistic history and offers lovely views across Paris. You can buy a studio apartment here for £60,000, but avoid the seedy area of Pigalle to the south.

Normandy

The lush green countryside and attractive coastal towns of Normandy that inspired Impressionist painters like Monet are easily accessible by ferry and car. The attractions of Paris are just a couple of hours' drive away too, making this region popular with British families. The climate of Normandy is slightly warmer than that of Kent or Sussex, but just as rainy! The cuisine is rich and creamy, consisting of Camembert cheese, fruity cider, Calvados, tripe and seafood. Property in Normandy is good value. A fully renovated traditional stone house with outbuildings and a swimming pool set in several acres of land can be bought for less than £100,000, or you can pick up a renovation property with several acres of land for less than £25,000.

Brittany

One in three properties in Brittany, in the north-west corner of France, is sold to British buyers. The north shore of this rugged maritime region is lined with magnificent beaches swept clean by the fierce tides, while the south coast is gentler and has a milder climate. The Bretons are a race of fishermen and farmers, and the land is steeped in Celtic myth, culture and tradition. This region is also famous for its fabulous oysters, lobster, shrimps and crabs, and delicious filled crêpes. Property in the ancient seaside towns of St Malo, Quimper and Dinard is expensive, but it is possible to pick up a pretty two-bedroom Breton farmhouse in a rural location just thirty minutes' drive away from Mont St Michel and the coast for just £65,000.

Poitou-Charentes

Many Francophiles consider the west Atlantic coast of France to have the best climate in the country. The region of Poitou-Charentes, south of the Loire, is totally unspoilt and enjoys almost as many hours of sunshine as the Côte d'Azur. It is one of the most peaceful parts of France, full of rolling farmlands, vineyards and long sandy beaches. La Rochelle is a delightful fishing town, and further inland is the town of Cognac, famous for its brandy. It is possible to pick up a chalet-style three-bedroom detached house with a large garden and swimming pool in a quiet Charente village for £140,000, but this previously undiscovered region looks set to become a bit of a hotspot in 2004, and prices are rising.

Languedoc-Rousillon

Along the south coast, the Catalan region of Langue doc-Rousillon borders the Pyrenees to the west, Spain and Andorra to the south, and Provence and the Cote d'Azur to the north-east. This popular area was undervalued for years, but the introduction of cheap flights to Carcassone, Toulouse and Montpellier mean prices have tripled in areas near the towns and coast, though it is possible to pick up a restored six-bedroom house in one of the villages closer to the Pyrenees for £110,000. The Languedoc region is situated between the sea and mountains, and if you select your location wisely, it is perfectly possible to go skiing in the morning, and swimming in the sea in the afternoon. The pace of life here is slow, and shops remain closed on Sundays. There are state-funded language courses for those who wish to improve their French, and most people who settle in the Languedoc attempt to integrate into their new community.

The trials and joys of renovating a derelict barn among the lavender fields and almond groves of Provence do not need to be extolled any further. The 'Peter Mayle' effect has turned this south-east corner of France into one of the most commercialised and colonised in the country. The area is overrun with tourists shopping for vegetables in the local markets during the summer. Any remaining wrecks have been snapped up long ago, and property prices are now almost on a par with those of Paris. Carolyn Wright Freeman, founding designer of the womenswear label Episode, paid £600,000 for an 1870s farmhouse close to the charming medieval town of Uzes, near Avignon. But if you are on a tighter budget, you can pick up a renovated barn with four bedrooms, wine cellar and swimming pool for half the price.

The Riviera

A villa or apartment in the right area of Cannes will produce an attractive letting income during the annual film festival. A four-bedroom villa with swimming pool and tennis courts, overlooking the bay of St Tropez, can cost over a million. However, if you are simply looking for a sunny bolthole on the Riviera that you can lock up and leave at the end of the summer, you can pick up a one-bedroom apartment with sea views and a balcony in the centre of Nice for £150,000.

Rest of the country

To the west, the Alpine regions of Savoy and Dauphine offer glorious scenery and plenty of sporting opportunities in summer and winter alike, while the stately Loire region in central France, the area of Burgundy and the Dordogne, the historic and gastronomic heart of France, have always been firm favourites with the British. And if you are looking to escape from your fellow expats altogether, there are still numerous other delightful areas in the Hexagon waiting to be discovered – just don't go looking for a British estate agent!

The buying process

The sale of a property in France is conducted by a *notaire,* an independent and highly trained government official. Once you have found a property, you will need to contact a local *notaire* to prepare a legally binding purchase agreement called a *compris de vente.* This will record the agreement to buy and sell between the vendor and purchaser, spell out the precise details of what is being sold, and stipulate the purchase price, deposit and any additional fees.

Your *notaire* will carry out certain searches on the property, round up all the documents he needs to complete the sale, and request for funds to be released from your lender. But he will *not* investigate planning proposals for the local area. You should also note that unlike British lenders who insist on carrying out a valuation survey before advancing a loan, French mortgages are *not* dependent on any structural surveys being carried out.

So in addition to engaging a *notaire,* you should also employ your own English-speaking lawyer to check that there are no plans to build a motorway behind your rural *gîte*, and a surveyor, to provide a full report on the structure of the property, before signing on the dotted line. Many UK surveyors operate in France, and if you are borrowing money from the foreign arm of a British bank, they should be able to recommend one.

The *compris de vente* will state clearly that the vendor is not responsible for any defects on the property you are buying, so you will have no legal comeback if you fail to commission your own survey. The contract will also specify a date for completion. Upon signing, you will have to pay your deposit – if you pull out of the sale after this, you will forfeit your deposit and you may even be sued by the vendor for any losses he has incurred.

On completion day, the seller's *notaire* will receive the balance of the purchase price and all other fees either by certified cheque, or directly into his bank account. If your money is coming from the UK, it may take several days for the transfer to be completed, so be sure to organise your funds in good time. As when buying a property in the UK, you should also ensure that you have buildings and contents insurance in place before taking the property into your possession.

Once all the necessary work has been completed, your *notaire* will draw up an *acte de vente* to complete the transfer of the property. You will then be issued with an *attestation* – a certificate to prove you are the owner of the property. The title deeds remain with the *notaire*, although you should be given a copy within six weeks.

Buying a property in France can be expensive. *Notaires'* fees range from 2 per cent to 3 per cent of the purchase price for a new property, to up to 8 per cent for an old one. On top of this there will also be tax to pay (up to 19.6 per cent on a new property), stamp duty, land registration fees, and your own survey and lawyer's fees. As in the UK, the process of purchasing a property can be slow and take up to three months in total.

Italy

While it is perfectly possible to remortgage a home that has soared in value in the UK, and buy a second property in Normandy or Charente with cash, it is simply not possible to do this in the honeypots of Italy.

Property in the most favoured region, Tuscany, is old, expensive and in short supply. A large roofless stone farm-house without gas, water and electricity will cost at least £150,000 to purchase and the same amount again to renovate and decorate. Property on the island of Venice is among the most expensive in the world, particularly if it overlooks the Grand Canal. Even an apartment in a good area of Milan or Rome can cost the same as a flat in London.

Buying property in Italy as a foreigner is a slow and complex business, and there are very few purpose-built resorts catering for international buyers looking for 'a little piece of England in the sun', so property here tends to attract sophisticated, upmarket buyers who love the art and music, the Renaissance, coffee, pasta, wine and magnificent scenery of this delightful country.

The regions, properties and prices

The British have been buying property in Tuscany and Umbria since the 1960s, and an estimated 10,000 Brits now own homes in 'Chiantishire'. Tuscany is one of the largest regions in Italy, and a land of mountains, olive groves, small hill towns, rolling countryside and white beaches. It also has history and art: the eternal cities of Florence, Pisa and Siena are all located here.

Although one Tuscan hill can look pretty much the same as another, location is important. A secluded property that is four hours' drive away from the airport, and half a mile up a track only suitable for goats, will test your patience in winter, and be difficult to let in summer. You should also consider the property's aspect: the dream Tuscan dwelling will have an east-facing terrace so that you can soak up the morning sun while you eat your breakfast, and a west-facing one so that you can watch it fall as you sip your glass of Montepulciano in the evening!

Tuscan summers may be glorious, but winters are cold and bitter, so a property protected by hills to the rear will shelter you from the piercing north winds. Properties made of grey hard stone will weather better over the years than those made of brown, sandy stone. Buying and renovating an old Tuscan farmhouse may be expensive, but should also be a good investment. Provided you buy in a good location, renovate to a high standard, and install the obligatory swimming pool, you should have no problem letting the property in summer. Many of the best Tuscan farmhouses are booked up years in advance for July and August.

If you find yourself priced out of Tuscany, you may be able to find something in neighbouring Umbria, although prices here are rising fast too. The landscape of Umbria is similar to that of Tuscany, minus the coastline. The region has two main towns: Perugia, which hosts an international jazz festival every summer, and Assisi, the birthplace of Italy's patron saint, St Francis. Florence, Pisa and Bologna are within driving distance too. At the time of writing, a three-bedroom house in a hilltop hamlet was available for renovation for £75,000.

If you are looking for value for money, head east of Umbria to the region of La Marche. Many consider this region to be the country's best-kept secret. The scenery is magnificent, and there are numerous fascinating towns to explore, the most famous being Urbino, the birthplace of Raphael. Property in the Marches is cheaper than in Tuscany and Umbria, consisting of elegant palazzos, white stone cottages and farmhouses suitable for renovation. You should be able to pick up something for under £110,000.

The car-free island of Venice, off the north-east coast of the region of Veneto, is divided into six *sestieri* (districts). A two-bedroom apartment on the Grand Canal near the Rialto Bridge will set you back at least £450,000, though you can find cheaper property in the outer districts of Castello to the east of San Marco, and Cannaregio to the north.

The western district of Dorsodoro, which houses the Accademia Galleries and Peggy Guggenheim museum, bustles with lively cafés and leafy piazzas, and is popular with British and American buyers. Property here is expensive, but deemed to be more secure than in other *sestieri*. The word *dorsoduro* means 'hard back' in Italian, and this district was built on elevated islands of heavy clay subsoil so the buildings are less likely to sink. But regardless of which *sestiere* you opt for, only buy property above the ground floor, and remember that all your furniture and belongings – and building materials too if you need to carry out renovation works – will have to be transported by boat!

Foreign buyers have tended to stick to the more economically dynamic northern and central regions of Italy rather than the more depressed and politically unstable south. But adventurous bargain-seekers might want to consider buying in the region of Puglia, located in the 'heel of Italy's boot'. This is Italy's major olive and wheat-growing area and offers mountains, forests and beaches. You can pick up a renovation property here for a few thousand pounds, but as the region is less well known than Tuscany and Umbria, it may be difficult to let it in summer.

The buying process

Buying a home in Italy can be an infuriatingly slow and bureaucratic process. Things will get done eventually, but never before one too many agitated phone calls and heated visits between all parties, so fulfilling your dream of owning a rustic Tuscan farmhouse or a resplendent Venetian apartment is likely to require considerable reserves of patience.

As in France, the legal transfer of a property must be done before a government-appointed notary, but you should employ a bilingual British lawyer to look after your interests. As soon as you have found a property, commission a survey, and ensure that your lawyer investigates all local planning proposals and checks that the property conforms with local planning and building regulations.

If you are satisfied that there is nothing untoward, you will need to sign a *compromesso* (preliminary contract) which can be drawn up by the estate agent, vendor, notary or lawyer. This will specify the terms of the sale, details of the property, the buyer and the seller, and the completion date. It will also give details of any conditions that have to be completed before the sale takes place.

Completion usually takes place within six to eight weeks, though some purchases can take up to four months. Upon signing the *compromesso*, you will have to pay your deposit. Be sure that you understand the terms under which this money will be refunded – typically, if you pull out of the sale, you will forfeit the money; but if the vendor pulls out, they will have to compensate you with double the sum.

Before the sale can be completed, you will have to obtain an Italian tax code (*codice fiscale*). You should also visit the property again with your lawyer to make sure it is in the condition you saw it in when you made your offer, and that it includes everything you agreed to buy in your *compromesso*.

Completion must take place face-to-face in front of an appointed notary. If you are not fluent in Italian, either an officially accredited interpreter must be present, or you must give power of attorney to your lawyer. You will have to pay the balance of the purchase price, plus all relevant taxes and *notaio*'s fees must be paid, and sign a legal transfer document (*atto di compravendita*) before the property becomes yours.

The notary will then register the new title deed at the Land Registry, and you should collect a copy from his office a week later. This is of paramount importance, as until the property has been registered in your name, you are not the legal owner. Total fees for buying a property in Italy are usually between 8 per cent and 15 per cent, consisting of stamp duty, notary fees and the surveyor's fees. Estate agents' fees are usually split between the buyer and seller too, so it is important that you only buy from an estate agent registered with the local Chamber of Commerce.

Spain

According to *Homes Overseas* magazine, Spain is the preferred destination for 42 per cent of Britons seeking a home abroad, and more than 650,000 Brits now own property in Spain. Hot summers and mild winters, combined with the well-developed infrastructure of international schools, shops, golf courses, healthcare and English-speaking estate agents and relocation consultants, make a property on the Spanish Costas a popular choice for those seeking a place in the sun without venturing too far out of their comfort zone.

Inland, the stylish cities of Barcelona and Madrid have large expatriate communities, great shopping, nightlife and culture, and make a great destination for a weekend break.

Meanwhile, those seeking the rural tranquillity of the real Spain need only drive an hour or so away from the coasts to the sleepy white Moorish villages clinging to the orange and lemon groves, awe-inspiring mountains of Sierra Nevada and Cabrera, and the wide open plains of the Alpujarras.

The regions, properties and prices

The Costa del Sol, on the south coast of Andalusia, is the most popular region with British buyers. Andalusia is the second largest region in Spain, and combines fabulous scenery and a great climate with all those things we commonly associate with Spain: tapas, sherry, bullfighting and flamenco. Inland, the region has three main towns: Seville, the romantic capital of Andalusia and birthplace of the myth of Don Juan; Granada, famous for its Moorish Alhambra Palace; and Cordoba.

British buyers account for over 80 per cent of transactions on many developments along the Costa del Sol, and it is fair to say that you could live here without ever speaking a word of Spanish or touching a paella if you didn't want to, so this is not the place to come if you seek peace and quiet, and want to discover the real Spain.

But the Costa del Sol is no longer cheap. Shortage of development land means property prices in the more popular towns are now on a par with those in England, and are predicted to continue rising as demand for homes shows little sign of abating. As standards have improved, the cost of living has risen too. As one newspaper reported, 'the cheap days of the Costa del Sol have had their chips'.

The chic resort of Marbella, where royalty and celebrity meet, has always been expensive. A two-bedroom apartment in a good location will cost at least £250,000. Other popular enclaves along this 154-kilometre stretch of coastline are the city of Malaga, which houses a new Picasso museum and many historic sites; the pretty town of Nerja to the east, which has retained its rustic character; the coastal town of Benalmadena; and the resorts of Calahonda and Riviera, where you can pick up a fully furnished three-bedroom, three-bathroom apartment, with terraces and pool, for £155,000.

The Costa Blanca, on the south-east region of Valencia, is another firm favourite with the British. Cheap concrete hotel blocks, fish & chip shops and English pubs still blight hideous towns like Benidorm to the south, but resorts to the north are clean, quiet and upmarket. Again, there is a well-established infrastructure to cater for foreigners; and property prices here now rival those on the Costa del Sol.

If you are priced out of the Costa del Sol and Costa Blanca, try the up-and-coming regions of Costa Calida, south of the Costa Blanca, and the Costa d'Almeria, which links Costa Calida with the Costa del Sol. Property in these regions currently costs 15–20 per cent less than on the sister Costas. If you are seeking more peace and quiet, head west for the Costa de la Luz, which stretches from the Portuguese border to Gibraltar, where the Costa del Sol begins.

This stunning coastline is protected by national parks, so construction is strictly controlled. The scenery inland is magnificent with mountains, rolling hills, citrus groves and quaint villages where time seems to have stood still. It is possible to pick up three-bedroom houses here for under £100,000, although with at least one estate agent in this region marketing properties in his office in the UK, the area looks unlikely to escape the British invasion for long.

The city of Barcelona, in the north-east region of Catalonia, is famous for its pavement cafés, winding streets, extravagant architecture and proximity to the beaches of Costa Brava, and attracts a young, hip crowd. This is the most expensive city in Spain, though it is possible to buy a studio flat for £80,000. With the UK just an hour and a half away by plane, an apartment in this stylish, cosmopolitan city would make a cool weekend crash pad, or a first home.

Property prices in the capital city of Madrid rose by 30 per cent in 2003, but generally homes are still slightly cheaper than in Barcelona. In January 2004, it was possible to purchase a one-bedroom flat beside the Plaza de Espana in the heart of the city for £105,000, though a large three-bedroom apartment in the upmarket district of Salamanca will set you back nearly £1 million.

You do not have to drive too far inland to discover the real Spain. Rural Andalusia is famous for its olive and almond farming, and the national parks north of Malaga, which are full of river valleys and picturesque lakes, are only an hour away from the city's airport. In October 2003, a four-bedroom, two-bathroom house with a roof terrace, set in olive groves, with a large garden, in the village of Iznajar was on sale for £110,000, or you could have bought a 100-year-old Spanish *finca* (farmhouse) with an acre of land, suitable for renovation, for £148,000. Expats who have bought property in the Andalusian countryside say the tranquillity and easy-going pace of life here is akin to life in England in the 1950s.

The Spanish islands

The three main Balearic Islands of Ibiza, Mallorca and Menorca have become very popular with the smart set in recent years. Last year, the comedian Jasper Carrott bought a five-bedroom villa in Camp de Mar, north of Palma in Mallorca for £2.6 million. The island's other celebrity denizens include Michael Douglas and Catherine Zeta-Jones, Claudia Schiffer, and the singer Annie Lennox. Property on the magical island of Ibiza has always been expensive. A cliffside villa with sea views will cost at least £700,000, though you can pick up a renovation property inland for about £200,000.

Although summers on the Balearic Isles are wonderfully hot, winters can be cold and wet. The islands shut down from late October to March, and even the charter flights dry up, so if you are seeking year-round sunshine, head for the Canary Islands.

The quiet island of Lanzarote has the most striking landscape of all the Canary Islands, and enforces stringent building restrictions – properties over two storeys high cannot be erected anywhere. There are also strictly zoned areas where no new developments can be built at all, so the island is comparatively unspoilt, and old *fincas* in the countryside are highly sought after.

Other popular areas are the south and east regions of the island, which have the best weather conditions and are close to the airport. Prices in Lanzarote are on a par with those in the cheaper areas of the Spanish mainland, and you can pick up a three-bedroom seafront villa with swimming pool and tennis courts for £242,000.

The buying process

As in France and Italy, a local notary will perform the legal transfer of the property in Spain, but it is essential to employ an English-speaking lawyer who is registered in Spain and fully conversant with the Spanish system. Newspapers and television programmes abound with sorry stories of naïve, inexperienced buyers who have bought properties without a legal title or planning permission, properties sold with missing infrastructure, homes sold to more than one buyer, and even homes that don't exist.

As I said earlier, when you buy a property in Spain, you inherit any debts, and also unpaid taxes and community charges. Although it is easy for your lawyer to check the property has no outstanding charges, it is virtually impossible to stop a seller from taking out a loan on the property after you have made the checks, and then disappearing. Another common practice is for the vendor to understate the purchase price of the property to reduce his capital gains tax liability.

The first thing to do if you want to buy a home in Spain is to obtain an identification number, known as a *numero de identificación de extranjero* (NIE). Without this, you will not be able to open a Spanish bank account, or arrange credit; you will also need this number to pay taxes. Once your lawyer has conducted searches to ensure that you are buying what you think you are buying, both in terms of property and the surrounding land, and that there are no debts or building restrictions on the land, you will need to sign a private contract (*contrato privado de compraventa*) and pay the deposit.

The Spanish system is slow, and completion usually takes place three or four months later, in front of the notary, when you (or your power of attorney) will sign the final deed (*escritura de compraventa*). After the payment of the balance of the purchase prices and fees have been made, the notary will pass you a copy of the *escrita* and the keys, and register the change of title at the Land Registry. This can take up to another three months.

Buying off-plan is very popular in Spain, but can present a myriad of problems, as it is very common to discover that the finished property, communal services and infrastructure (roads, parking areas, swimming pools, landscaping, tennis courts, telephone services) are not as described in the contract. If you are buying an unfinished property, you will be making payments in agreed stages and should ensure that the contract allows you to withhold the final payment until six to twelve months after the work has been completed, so you can call the builders back if necessary.

Portugal

The sun-kissed beaches, warm, friendly people, gentle pace of life and year-round temperate climate of Portugal have been welcoming British visitors for centuries, and sophisticated property developments on the west coast of Estremadura, near the capital city of Lisbon, and along the ever-popular Algarve, are now attracting increasing numbers of second-home buyers.

Portugal is one of the smallest countries in Europe. Situated on the far west side of the mainland, it shares a border with Spain to the east and has a Mediterranean feel, but enjoys a more upmarket image than the Costas. With its numerous golf courses, tennis academies, sailing clubs and fine opportunities for windsurfing, Portugal has always been popular with sports' enthusiasts, and has been dubbed 'Sportugal'. Celebrities with homes in the Algarve include Sir Cliff Richard and footballer Michael Owen. A luxury three-bedroom villa with a swimming pool, an acre of land and views of the coast can cost £750,000, though it is possible to buy a family home in a fishing town on the western Algarve for £250,000.

The regions, properties and prices

Much of the central and eastern areas of the Algarve, which have been attracting package holiday companies and expatriate buyers since the 1980s, are now achingly over-developed. The former fishing town of Albufeira is now a sprawling city which has retained some of its original character, and a new marina is under construction. Cheap studio flats and one-bedroom apartments can be bought for under £80,000. At the luxury end of the market, a Moorish-style two-bedroom apartment in the prestigious resorts of Quinta da Logo and Vale do Logo, which offer championship golf courses, tennis academies, swimming pools, health clubs, bars and discos, will set you back at least £250,000.

The western Algarve is altogether much quieter and offers dramatic beaches, rugged coastline and huge swathes of unspoilt countryside. The coastline between the Moorish town of Lagos and ancient maritime port of Sagre on the western tip of the country has some particularly fine beaches and is becoming increasingly popular with affluent British families.

In 2002, Jo Wheeler, a weather presenter for Sky television, and her husband bought a four-bedroom family house with a pool and terrace in the laid-back cosmopolitan fishing village of Praia da Luz for £200,000. Their four children now attend nearby English-speaking international schools, and Jo commutes to London every Friday to work weekend shifts.

Other villages in this region include the small market town of Monchique perched high on the beautiful hills of the Serra de Monchique; the inland village of Caldas de Monchique, which is famous for its thermal spa waters; and the main market town of Loule, which is set around a thirteenth-century castle.

The sophisticated and vibrant city of Lisbon is built upon seven hills and is just half an hour away from the coast. The resort towns of Estoril, which has one of the largest casinos in Europe, Cascais and Sintra have for centuries tempted royalty and aristocracy to build palaces and mansions, and the region is becoming known as the 'Portuguese Riviera'. It is still possible, though, to buy a two-bedroom flat with sea views in a fashionable area of the city for under £80,000.

Although property prices along the coasts are rising, it is not yet advisable to venture too far out into the remote areas of Portugal to find a bargain to renovate. Unlike France and Spain, which have excellent road and rail networks, the infrastructure in Portugal is less developed, remote country regions are poorly served by road, and housing can be primitive.

The buying process

Buying a property in Portugal can be a slow and difficult process, and is one that is subject to change, so ensure you employ a lawyer who is fully versed in UK and Portuguese law. As in Spain, you will need to obtain a fiscal number (*numero de contribuinte*). Your lawyer should check there are no outstanding debts, or restrictive covenants on the property. He should also confirm with the Land Registry (*Conservatorio do Registo Predial*) that the property has been registered in the vendor's name. If a property has not been passed on through a will, the whole family may be entitled to a share of it, and come knocking on your door claiming their portion of your home in future years!

The preliminary contract (*Contrato Promesso de Compra a Venda*) is drawn up by the seller's representative, and as well as containing a description of the property and confirmation of the buyers' and sellers' identities, should also include a 'clear title' of ownership. The seller should also provide a habitation licence for any property built after 1951, and also a *cardetta*, which confirms that all debts relating to the property have been paid. Upon signing this contract, you will pay your deposit and, as in Italy, if you withdraw from the sale you will forfeit the money, but if the vendor pulls out, he will be liable for double the deposit.

The second stage of the purchase is the signing of the conveyance document (*escritura*), in the presence of the notary. The notary will read out the contract before the buyer and seller, vet the preliminary contract, and take the balance of the purchase price, plus all related fees and taxes. The property will then be transferred into your name. Having bought the property, it is your responsibility to register it with the Land Registry, by submitting a copy of the *escritura* to the Inland Revenue.

Many people buying a home in Portugal do so through an offshore company. There are many fiscal advantages to doing this – you will be exempt from property transfer tax, capital gains tax and inheritance tax, and there will be no conveyancing costs either, as the property will simply be transferred to the new owner. However, there will be a one-off fee to set up an offshore company, plus annual management fees, and you should take independent financial advice if you are planning to go down this route.

The USA: Florida and New York

Florida

More than 50,000 Brits have bought property in the sunshine state of Florida. From the theme park mecca of south Orlando, to the exquisite boutiques of Palm Beach in the Everglades, and the art deco hotels, eclectic music scene and sizzling nightlife of Miami Beach, this southern state offers something for everyone.

The strength of the pound means that property in Florida is excellent value. Communications both within the state and to other parts of the USA and the UK are excellent, and the standard of living and service is high. It is possible to buy a three-bedroom villa with swimming pool and double garage just thirty minutes' away from Disney World for under £150,000, or a two-bedroom, two-bathroom waterfront apartment in North Miami for £65,000.

New York

But if you are looking to buy a slice of the Big Apple, it is a very different story. The return of big Wall Street bonuses and the lowest interest rates in the USA for forty years mean property prices on the island of Manhattan have soared beyond belief, and the average two-bedroom apartment now sells for $1.028 million (£539,300). However, there are no restrictions for Brits wanting to buy, and property transactions in New York can be completed far quicker than in many parts of Europe. So, if you have the money and want a pad in the city that never sleeps, just bring your chequebook and passport, and you can be living like a real-life *Sex and the City* character in just sixty days.

The regions, properties and prices

It is hard to believe that the city of Orlando, home to Mickey Mouse, Disney World and Universal Studios, was once a quiet farming town. Situated deep in the heart of Orange County, the south part of the city boasts ninety different theme parks. However, it is not all about 'extra large fries' and 'have a nice day'. To the north of the city, farming replaces tourism, and the Silver Springs and Ocala National Forest provide opportunities for canoeing, hiking, swimming and cave-diving.

Daytona Beach, home to the J F Kennedy Space Center, is just an hour's drive from Orlando. A few miles south of Space Coast is Cocoa Beach, a surfer's paradise and a great vantage point from which to see space launches. Nearly 70 per cent of Brits who have bought property in Florida have settled in Orlando. If you are looking for a home that is ready to move into from day one, many real-estate brokers offer a 'turnkey package', which means you can buy the property fully furnished, right down to the linen, DVD player and cutlery, and have the property customised to suit your own needs.

Palm Beach in the Everglade region of Florida is one of America's ritziest resorts, and is the most exclusive part of the sunshine state. It is home to the bestselling author James Patterson, and his wife and young son, Jack. Rod Stewart and the Kennedy clan also have residences here. The entry price for a two-bedroom, two-bathroom apartment is about £250,000. Closer to Worth Avenue, the area's main shopping street bristling with exclusive names such as Cartier, Chanel, Gucci and Armani, prices start at £443,000.

Two hours' south of Palm Beach is the hip, multicultural city of Miami, one of the most stylish holiday destinations in the USA. Coconut Grove, once an enclave for struggling writers and artists, is now one of the most fashionable parts of this hedonistic city. It still has a Bohemian atmosphere, though the arrival of trendy boutiques, art galleries and pavement cafés mean that penniless creative types can no longer afford to live there.

Miami Beach is connected to the mainland by numerous causeways, and is where the beautiful people and movie moguls hang out. Its white sandy coastline has been voted one of the top ten beaches in the world, while the pastel-coloured art deco hotel and apartment blocks that line the streets of South Beach are world famous.

Away from the blue skies and white beaches of Florida, to the high-brow culture, shopping, theatres and skyscrapers of New York City, a three-bedroom flat with unobstructed views of Central Park costs £3 million.

The hottest place to buy in Manhattan in early 2004 was TriBeCa, the 'triangle below Canal Street', renowned for its beautiful loft apartments and great restaurants, including the celebrity favourite, Nobu. Warehouse conversions here are spacious, the area is quiet and upscale and, many believe, still undervalued. But if you are looking for a real bargain, head for Harlem, where you can get a sizeable apartment taking up the entire floor of a Manhattan brownstore for the price of a shoebox downtown. However, if you are looking to rent a place for six months, the Upper East Side, a traditionally expensive area, is currently offering some of the best bargains in the city.

The buying process

From a legal point of view, the USA is one of the safest places to buy property, and the buying process is far less convoluted than the British one. Although it is advisable to employ an independent lawyer, particularly if you are a foreigner, the estate agency business (known as realtors) is much more highly regulated than in the UK, and legalities are handled by 'title companies', so it is normal for property transactions to be completed without the need for lawyers.

Ensure that any realtor you employ holds a Florida Real Estate Commission license (FREC) or its local equivalent in other states, as holders of this certificate are obliged to act under a code of conduct and you can be reimbursed if you suffer losses as a result of unprofessional behaviour, even though the realtor's fees are paid by the seller. Your realtor will show you around properties, submit your offer to the vendor's agent, and draw up a contract, subject to any conditions, such as a survey, a termite inspection if you are buying a resale property, or a mortgage offer. The contract will also state how the final balance (known as closing costs) are to be paid, and specify exactly what is being sold. When you are satisfied with the contract, you sign it and pay your deposit.

The final part of the sale is handled by the title company, which is similar to an insurance company. They will check that the property has a clear title, and that it carries no debts, restrictions or easements. You should visit the property again before completion to check that it satisfies everything in the contract. Completion of the sale takes place in a meeting between the title company, buyer, seller, realtor, lawyer and representative of the mortgage company or bank. Once you have signed the contract, and the balance has been transferred to the vendor, you will be given the keys to your home.

In addition to legal and title company fees, you should also budget for mortgage tax (there are two types of tax levied on mortgages in Florida: documentary stamps and intangible tax); and also an annual property tax, similar to council tax in the UK. If you let your property for more than fourteen days, you must file a US tax return and pay tax on rental income, although this can be offset against mortgage costs. You should also beware of local restrictions on letting property. Many counties in the state will not permit you to let a property for less than six months. There may also be certain community restrictions that forbid you to hang washing outside, or paint the exterior of your home a certain colour.

Summary

The property goddess only buys property in a country towards which she feels a genuine emotional pull. She plans her finances carefully, taking currency exchange rates into account, and familiarises herself with the buying procedure and real estate laws of the country in which she is buying before starting to search for a property.

1) Research the area, properties available, buying procedures, real estate laws and tax regimes for the country in which you are buying. You can never know enough when buying a property abroad.

2) Arrange an 'inspection trip' to view properties. Plan your

viewings from the UK, to ensure you stick to a schedule. Once out there, talk to local estate agents, shopkeepers, builders, and other foreigners who have bought there.

3) When you have found a property, buy all the currency you will need to complete the purchase. If you do not have the money upfront, reserve the money at the prevailing rate. Do not gamble on currency exchange markets.

4) Employ a good English-speaking lawyer.

5) Open a bank account in the country in which you are buying, and always have sufficient cash reserves in foreign currency and sterling.

7

Renting

For most readers of this book, renting will be a short-term solution. Nevertheless, there are times when it is more sensible than buying. As we have seen, buying property involves some complicated decision-making. If you are relocating to a different part of the country, or buying property abroad, renting for a few months gives you an opportunity to find your feet in unknown territory, and generally fine-tune your criteria.

Renting to buy

Another growing trend is 'renting to buy'. This is particularly popular when house prices are rising rapidly month by month, and homeowners are keen to cash in on the boom by selling their home when prices are at a premium, then renting for a few months, and buying their next home when the market has come off the boil. Although it is difficult to get the timing absolutely right (prices may continue to rise over the next six or twelve months, rather than fall, and you will end up paying more for your next home than if you had bought when you sold), the advantage is that this will allow you more time to search for your next home. You will be in a much stronger position to make an offer because you will have nothing to sell and the purchase will be chain-free at your end. Homeowners stuck in a chain have even been known to move into a caravan if they cannot complete on the purchase of their next home, rather than risk losing their buyer and breaking the chain below them.

Finding a rental property

The best way to find a rental property in the UK is through a lettings agent who is a member of the Association of Residential Lettings Agents (ARLA). As I explained in Chapter 5, ARLA is the professional body for the residential lettings market, and holds separate client accounts, so your deposit money will be safe, and your tenancy agreement will comply with all the latest legislation.

Before drawing up an agreement, the agent will make checks with credit reference agencies and your employer to verify that you are able to meet the rental payments.

Be wary of renting a property through classified adverts in newspapers or shop windows, particularly if you are a single woman. It is not unknown for landlords who have defaulted on their mortgages to advertise their properties to let, collect a deposit and the first month's rent, and then for the property to be repossessed.

Tenancy agreements

Tenancy agreements are now either assured shorthold or assured longhold tenancies. The typical shorthold tenancy is for an initial period of six months, although since the introduction of a new Housing Act in the spring of 1997, they can be for a shorter period. In either case, the property automatically reverts to the landlord at the end of the agreement, although the lease can be renewed if the landlord agrees.

Tenancy agreements are legally binding between the landlord and yourself, and should state: the full address of the property to be let; the name and address of the landlord and letting agent; the length of the lease; amount of rent payable; the rights and responsibilities of the landlord and tenant; bills you are responsible for paying; any restrictions – such as not keeping pets on the property, not using the address to advertise a business, and not playing loud music after a certain hour; and security requirements, such as not leaving the property empty for longer than a certain period of time.

There are also likely to be numerous other clauses that you should read carefully before signing. In particular, look out for a clause that stipulates that the landlord is not liable for any injury to the tenant or their guests, even if caused by a default on the premises. As we saw in Chapter 5, landlords are legally obliged to ensure the gas and electrics are safe, and that furniture complies with fire safety regulations, and you can bring a civil claim against the landlord if you suffer an injury due to negligence in these areas.

Inventories

If you rent through an ARLA agent, they will arrange for an independent firm to take an inventory at the start of the tenancy and at the end. The landlord usually pays for the first inventory and the tenant pays for the final one.

The inventory should include a listing of all furniture, fittings, linen, crockery and other items in the property, and also their condition at the beginning of the lease. Check this carefully; if there are stains on the carpets, the curtains have not been washed, or scratches or water marks on furniture, these should be noted, or you may find yourself billed for repair when you leave.

Bills and contents insurance

Landlords normally pay water rates, but you will have to pay council tax, gas, electricity and telephone bills. You should make a note of meter readings the day you move in and the day you move out, so you are not billed for any usage before or after your tenancy period began. Your landlord should have adequate buildings insurance and cover for any furniture provided, but you should organise contents insurance for your own possessions.

Problems and complaints

The most common problems that tenants have with landlords when renting accommodation are landlords who are continually popping round to check on the property (or, worse, entering when you are not there); those who fail to attend to maintenance or repair problems, or ask you to sort them out even when they are not your responsibility; and landlords who fail to return the deposit. These are all more likely to occur when renting privately rather than through an established ARLA-registered agent.

Most tenancy agreements will state that you must inform your landlord or lettings agent immediately if there is any 'damage, disrepair, defect or deficiency' in the property. Emergency problems such as burst pipes or leaking washing machines should be attended to immediately. Do not organise your own tradesmen to put the problem right, or attempt to do it yourself, unless you have written permission from the landlord or agent to do so, and they have agreed to reimburse expenses.

If you lose your job, or become unable to pay the rent, inform your landlord or lettings agent of the situation immediately, as landlords can apply to the courts to claim unpaid rent and have you evicted from the premises after only two months.

Summary

Renting is usually a short-term solution, but is not without its problems.

1) Use an ARLA registered agent to find a rental property.

2) Ensure that a full inventory is taken when you move in. This is usually paid for by the landlord.

3) Make a note of meter readings the day you move in, and buy sufficient contents insurance.

4) Most tenancy agreements require you to give at least one month's notice when you want to leave. Tenants usually pay for the inventory when checking out.

Appendix

Architects

Royal Society of British Architects (RIBA)
020 7580 5533
www.riba.org

The Architects Registration Board
020 7580 5861
www.arb.org.uk

Architecture and Surveying Institute
01344 630798

Building Regulators

Federation of Master Builders
020 7608 5150
www.fmb.org.uk

House Builders Federation
020 7608 5100
www.hbf.co.uk

National House Building Council
01494 735363
www.nhbc.co.uk

Chartered Surveyors

Royal Institute of Chartered Surveyors
0870 333 1600
www.rics.org.uk

Royal Institute of Chartered Surveyors for Scotland
www.rics-scotland.org.uk

Conveyancing and Estate Agents

The National Association of Estate Agents
01926 496800
www.naea.co.uk

Council for Licensed Conveyancers
01245 349599

Government Bodies

Office of Deputy Prime Minister, Housing Private Sector
Division
www.housing.odpm.gov.uk

Office for the Ombudsman of Estate Agents
01722 333306
www.oea.co.uk

Gas Installation & Electrical Contractors

Electrical Contractors Association
020 7313 4800
www.eca.co.uk

CORGI (Council for Registered Gas Installers)
01256 372200
www.corgi-gas.com

Leaseholds

The Leasehold Advisory Service
020 7253 2043
www.lease-advice.org

Managing and Lettings Agents

Association of Residential Managing Agents
020 7978 2607
www.arma.org.uk

Association of Residential Letting Agents
0845 345 5752
www.arla.co.uk

Property Search Websites

www.easier.co.uk

www.findaproperty.com

www.fish4homes.co.uk

www.rightmove.co.uk

Private Sales

www.propertybroker.co.uk

Property Abroad

Conti Financial Services
01273 772811
www.overseasandukfinance.com

John Howell & Co
International Solicitors and Lawyers for Spain, France, Italy
and Portugal
020 7420 0400
www.legal21.org

Bennett and Co. Solicitors (property and inheritance work
overseas)
01625 586937
www.bennett-and-co.com

Index